1.50

Wales

IN

Industrial

Britain

c1760 – c1914

David Evans

D1550722

Hodder & Stoughton
A MEMBER OF THE HODDER HEADLINE GROUP

Acknowledgements

The cover shows, 'Testing a collier's lamp', by A Griffiths, courtesy of the Glynn Vivian Art Gallery, Swansea.

Image Select 4a; Hunting Aerofilms Limited 4b; Hampshire Record Office 4c (Q23/2/122/1), 41d (TOP 10/3/5); The Illustrated London News Picture Library 5f, 24a, 35b, 65e; Chepstow Museum 6a; Museum of Welsh Life 6b, 7c, 7d, 51d; Glamorgan Record Office 7e, 18a, 39e, 69f; Hulton Deutsch Collection Limited 8a, 18b, 40b, 49d, 66c, 68b; National Museum of Wales 9f, 20b, 28a, 53c (bottom); Architect of the Capitol 10b; Mansell Collection 11d, 16b, 25e, 31e, 38c, 39d, 54c, 56a, 57d, 61c, 63c, 64c, 65d, 79d; Science and Society Picture Library 12a, 12c; Hanley Museum and Art Gallery, Staffs./Bridgeman Art Library - Worcestershire willow-patterned plate (transfer printed), by Granger Lee and Company, c1850, Worcester 17f; Derby Mercury/Derby Local Studies Library 19e; Helmshore Local History Society 19f; National Library of Wales 20b, 21f, 50c, 63e, 75b; Cyfarthfa Castle Museum and Art Gallery 22b, 22d, 23g, 32a, 33h; Welsh Industrial and Maritime Museum 24b, 26a, 26b, 36a, 46b; Centris Coal Benifits Records Management Centre 27e; Gwynedd Archives Service 28b, 29e; Mary Evans Picture Library 20c, 30a, 46d, 74a; David Evans 34a, 44a, 52a, 53c (top), 54a, 70c, 73e; British Waterway Archives 37e; The Wellcome Trust 38a, 72c; National Library of Wales/The Robert Owen Memorial Museum 43d; Bristol Record Office (17562/1) 44c; Wilberforce House, Hull City Museums and Art Gallery 45d; Trevor May, The Victorian Schoolroom, Shire Publications Limited 48a; Mrs M Neil/Cardiff Yesterday, Volume 7, Stewart Williams Publications 51e; Newport Museum and Art Gallery, Gwent 58a (right), 59c; Victoria and Albert Museum 60, 61d; Royal Welch Fusiliers Regimental Museum, Caernarfon 62b; Trades Union Congress 67e; Coal Society. A History of the South Wales Mining Valleys 1840-1980, Gomer Press 68a; The Western Mail and Echo Limited 68a, 77e; by permission of the National Museum of Labour History 71e; Old Rhondda in Photographs, Stewart Williams Publications 76b (top); Cardiff Yesterday, Volume 17, Stewart Williams Publications 77d.

Every effort has been made to trace and acknowledge ownership of copyright. The publishers will be glad to make suitable arrangements with any copyright holders whom it has not been possible to contact.

British Library Cataloguing in Publication Data

A catalogue for this title is available from the British Library

ISBN   0340 64347 1

First published 1996
Impression number   10 9 8 7 6 5 4 3 2 1
Year   1999 1998 1997 1996

This book is published with the financial support of the Curriculum and Assessment Authority for Wales

Copyright © 1996 David Evans

All rights reserved. No part of this publication may be reproduced or transmitted in any form or by any means, electronic or mechanical, including photocopy, recording, or any information storage and retrieval system, without permission in writing from the publisher or under licence from the Copyright Licensing Agency Limited. Further details of such licences (for reprographic reproduction) may be obtained from the Copyright Licensing Agency Limited, of 90 Tottenham Court Road, London W1P 9HE.

Typeset by The University of Wales, Aberystwyth, Wales
Printed in Great Britain for Hodder & Stoughton Educational, a division of Hodder Headline Plc, 338 Euston Road, London NW1 3BH by Cambridge University Press, Cambridge

Contents

A time for change

In 1760 there were fewer than seven million people living in Wales and England. London was already a big city but Cardiff, with fewer than 2,000 people, was barely a small town. There were no factories or railways and it would be some time before homes had running water, gas and electricity.

In the countryside

In those days, most people lived in the countryside. They made their own clothes, grew their own food and kept animals. They used simple machines like spinning wheels and handlooms to make wool and cloth in their own homes. There were no farms as we know them today. Instead, the land around each village formed three large open fields. Each field was divided into strips and shared among the villagers. To prevent the land becoming exhausted, one field was left unused or **fallow** each year. Local people also kept a few animals, geese and chickens on the land they could use freely, the **common land**.

In the towns

The towns were places of business and trade. Here there were the shopkeepers, innkeepers and tradesmen. London, with its horse-drawn carriages and cabs, cobbled streets and pedlars shouting their wares, was a busy and noisy place. Most townsfolk were poor. They lived as best they could by doing odd jobs or, if they were down and out, by begging or stealing.

A A woman works at a spinning wheel in her own home

B An aerial photograph shows evidence of strip farming. Each ridge was supposed to have been the length a horse could pull a plough without a rest - a furrow-long or furlong

C An enclosure map shows how the commissioners shared out the land around the village of Horton Heath in Hampshire

The end of the old way of farming

The first big change came about in the countryside when landowners put hedges around their fields to enclose them. With more food needed to feed the growing number of people, farming was becoming more profitable. The old system was wasteful and besides, farmers wanted to try out new ideas. When the decision was taken to enclose the fields, the land was shared out by **commissioners**. Sadly, this led to a great deal of distress since many farmers could not afford to put hedges and fences around their land. They had no choice but to sell up and look for work in the towns. In some villages, even the land used freely by everyone, the common land, was enclosed.

The coming of machines

There were also other important changes taking place. The invention of new machines for spinning and weaving meant that the old system of making wool and cloth at home was coming to an end. To start with, water power was used to operate the new machines but this was soon to give way to steam-power. New buildings had to be built to house the machines. These were called factories or, in the textile industry, **mills**. The owners built rows of houses around their factories to provide homes for their workers. All these developments marked the start of what became known as the Factory Age.

In all the villages, there is shocking decay. The farm houses are not so many ... the labourers' houses disappear also. The enclosures are a waste ...

D In his book *Rural Rides*, William Cobbett wrote about the enclosures

The law arrests the man or woman
Who steals the goose from the common
But leaves the greater rascal loose,
Who steals the common from the goose.

E A popular rhyme of the day

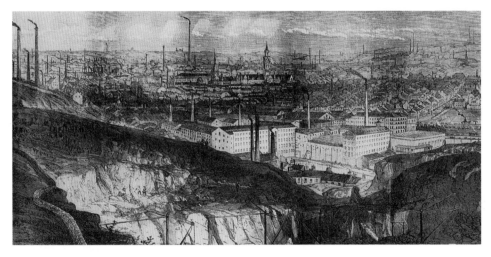

F *(left)* Things to come - textile mills in Bradford (1879)

1 Look at sources B and C. What changes might enclosures bring to the way the countryside looked?

2 'The changes which happened to farming were really what everyone wanted.' Using sources D and E and other information in this chapter, say whether you agree with this statement.

3 Using the information in this chapter, what changes would someone alive at that time notice about towns and the countryside if they were to come back today? Are there some things they would find that had not changed much?

$\mathcal{W}$ales 2oo years ago

No new roads had been built across the Welsh mountains since Roman times and those which existed were unkept and not suitable for carriages or coaches. This meant that Wales remained cut off from the outside world and, for a time, was little affected by events and changes elsewhere.

The Welsh countryside

Wales was mainly a land of villages and small farms and most people depended on agriculture for their livelihood. Few travelled beyond their own village. Their homes were stone-walled, **whitewashed** cottages with either thatched or slated roofs. Farming implements were very simple. Ploughs were made of wood with iron shares and leather flails, used for threshing. The most popular cart was the two-wheeled 'gambo'.

At shearing and harvest time, farmers came together to help each other. Life was hard with only market day and festivals like *Calan Mai* (May Day) and *Calan Gaeaf* (All Saint's Day) to look forward to. The hills provided good grazing for large flocks of sheep.

A Chepstow in 1812. Situated on the estuary of the River Wye, the town was the gateway to Wales

B A typical stone-walled Welsh cottage at Lampeter in Dyfed

C The inside of a one-roomed cottage at Rhostryfan in Gwynedd. The cottage dates from 1762

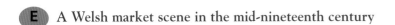

D A 'gambo'. An example of this type of cart, which was still in use well into the twentieth century, can be seen at the Museum of Welsh Life, St Fagans

E A Welsh market scene in the mid-nineteenth century

1 What clues are given in sources A and D as to how difficult travel was at this time?

2 Using sources B and C and other information in the text, briefly describe how comfortable you think life would be for the poorer people. You may, for example, want to refer to heating and lighting, materials they used and furniture.

Drovers, society and industry

The Drovers

Farmers depended on drovers to get their animals to market. Most were taken to the Midlands but some went as far as London. The drovers were important men since they were the country people's only contact with the outside world. When they returned they brought not only money, but also goods to purchase and news. Even among the Welsh people, drovers did not enjoy the best of reputations.

The few small towns of Wales

There were few towns of any size in Wales at this time. Some like Bala, Carmarthen, Cowbridge, Llandovery, Machynlleth and Tregaron owed their importance to the fact that they held regular markets. Cardigan, Chepstow, Haverfordwest and Swansea were ports involved in coastal trade.

Welsh high society

Families such as the Williams-Wynn of Wynnstay, the Gwyns of Llansannor and the Morgans of Tredegar were major landowners and leading figures in Welsh society. Sir Watkin Williams Wynn, who owned estates in Gwynedd, Clwyd and Powys was the greatest landowner in Wales. Members of the family had represented Denbighshire in Parliament for over 150 years!

   Beneath them were the gentry and country squires. Their wealth varied and they lived within the community. There were some small farmers who owned their land but most were **tenant farmers** who just rented a few hectares, or ordinary labourers who worked for a wage. The old Welsh rural way of life was not to last. The time was coming when many would leave the land and move to find better paid work in the ironworks and mines.

Industry

There had always been a number of small industries in Wales - small iron furnaces dependent on charcoal, cloth in the villages of the Teifi Valley, lead and silver mining in Dyfed and Clwyd and shipbuilding at Chepstow. In the years to come, industry was going to develop very quickly and turn the once forested valleys of Glamorgan and Gwent into one of the greatest iron and coal producing areas in the world.

A A drover at Smithfield market

He was a man of about forty years with a broad, red face … He was dressed in a pepper and salt coat, breeches of corduroy and brown boots.

B In *Wild Wales*, George Borrow describes a Welsh drover

C (right) The old Welsh clergyman and poet, Vicar Prichard, thought it necessary to tell drovers how to behave

If you're a drover deal honestly,
Pay correctly for what you've had,
Keep your word, don't break your promise,
Better be truthful than rich.

D The structure of Welsh society

Nobles
Gentry
Tenant farmers
Labourers

The old drover sleeps, his work completed:
Throughout his wasted life he cheated,
His world is now a narrow bed -
Fie! Let him cheat her instead!

E Twm o'r Nant didn't mince his words when he suggested a suitable verse for the headstone on a drover's grave

F An artist's impression of the Rhondda Valley at the start of the nineteenth century

1 (a) Why did drovers not enjoy a good reputation? Use sources A, C and E to help you.
  (b) Which of these three sources gives the most sympathetic view about drovers?
  (c) Why did you choose that particular source?

2 Does source F prove that the Rhondda Valley had no industry in the early nineteenth century?

3 Do the sources and other information in this chapter give you any clues about the role of women in Welsh society at this time?

3 *P*eople with new ideas

In Britain, the various classes of people lived very different lives. The landed gentry had splendid homes and were looked after by servants. Many were Members of Parliament who had a large say in the running of the nation's affairs. At the other end of the scale, working men owned no land and had few possessions. Without even the right to vote, they had no say in Parliament and had no means of changing things.

The loss of the American colonies

King George III was obstinate and made some very bad decisions. Needing money, his ministers decided to tax British colonists in North America. The colonists, who had no one to speak for them in Parliament in London, refused to pay and, in 1776, declared themselves free from British rule. Led by George Washington, the colonists fought for, and won, their independence. The loss of the American **colonies** was a blow to British pride.

The French Revolution

In France, the ordinary people had long suffered injustice as their king and his nobility enjoyed privileges, living idle and extravagant lives. By 1789, they had endured enough. They turned on Louis XVI, sweeping away the old system. During the French Revolution, the king and thousands of noblemen were sent to the **guillotine**.

What effect did these events have on the British people?

Some people in Britain supported what had happened in America and in France. They admired the American Declaration of Independence which said that all men had certain rights - 'life, liberty and the pursuit of happiness', and they supported the call of the French for '*Liberté, Egalité et Fraternité*' (Freedom, Equality and Brotherhood). **Radicals**, people who believed in trying to reform things by getting to the root cause of the problem, wanted change and some even urged the people to follow the example set by the French!

With good reason, the ruling classes feared the radicals and were worried that there might be unrest and riots. Edmund Burke, a politician, warned that revolutions were best avoided since they ruined the good work of past centuries and would only lead to more violence. Tom Paine, one of the most out-spoken radicals of his time, wanted to do away with the monarchy. He had fought for the colonists in America and had been in France during the Revolution.

> We hold these truths ... that all men are treated equal, that they are **endowed** by their Creator with ... certain rights, that among these are life, liberty, and the pursuit of happiness.

A The Declaration of Independence set out the beliefs of those who wished to break from British rule

B The signing of the American Declaration of Independence on 4 July 1776. The Declaration was written by Thomas Jefferson whose family originally came from North Wales

> *How much the greatest event that has happened in the world, and how much the best.*

C This is what Charles James Fox, a radical Member of Parliament, said of the French Revolution

Outspoken Welsh radicals

From London, four Welshmen expressed the views of their countrymen. Richard Price, a chapel minister from Bridgend, wrote a book backing the American colonists which so pleased them that he was invited to become an American citizen. He also wrote in support of the French Revolution. David Williams, another minister, held similar views. His popularity among the French Revolutionaries was such that they offered him French citizenship. John Jones, better known as *Jac Glan-y-gors*, ran an inn in London which was a popular meeting place for Welshmen in the city. In his books, he attacked the power of the king, the nobility and the clergy. The sale of his books was banned and he was forced to leave London and return to Wales. Another colourful character was a Baptist minister from Llanfabon, Morgan John Rhys. He went to France during the Revolution to try to give away Bibles. Back in Wales, he wrote about the suffering of working people. He emigrated and spent the rest of his days in America.

D A poster used at the time of the French Revolution

A share in two revolutions is living to some purpose.

E Tom Paine said this, looking back on his life

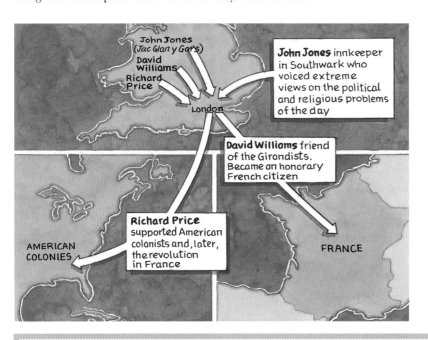

F (*left*) London-based Welsh radicals

1 (a) **Why might some people in Britain support what was happening in France and the United States? Sources A and B would be helpful in answering this question.**
   (b) **Do you think the ruling classes would have been enthusiastic about these two revolutions? Give reasons for your answer.**

2 **What impressions do you think source D is trying to give? How effective do you think it is?**

3 **Produce a brief speech either supporting or opposing radical change in Britain at this time.**

4 **How accurate and up-to-date do you think most people were in knowing about and understanding what was happening in France and the United States? You should refer to the information in this chapter and Chapters 1 and 2.**

Steam–power and the age of the machine

The story of Britain during the 100 years after 1760 is mainly an account of the changes which turned an agricultural country into an industrial one. These were years of discovery, invention and scientific progress which completely changed the face of the country and the everyday lives of the people.

Early water-powered machines

For centuries, the only forms of power had been human energy and that of animals, wind and water. Windmills and waterwheels had long been used to turn millstones and grind corn to flour. In the textile industry, Richard Arkwright made an important breakthrough when, in 1769, he invented a spinning machine which used running water to power it - a water-frame. Arkwright has been called 'the father of the factory system'. Even so, water-power was not the answer.

Thomas Newcomen

Thomas Newcomen was a blacksmith from Devon. In 1712, he built the first steam engine. It relied on steam and the pressure of the atmosphere to produce a pumping, up-and-down movement, and was used in mines to pump water. Newcomen's engine could not turn a wheel and so could not be used to operate machinery.

James Watt's steam engine

To turn a wheel, the steam engine had to have a circular or rotary motion. James Watt and his partner, Matthew Bolton, made this possible when they improved earlier steam engines. The new **rotary engine** could work pumps and drive machinery. Their engine was to provide the energy which made great industrial changes possible.

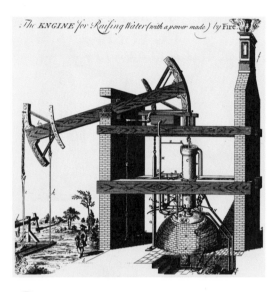

The ENGINE for Raising Water (with a power made) by Fire

A Newcomen's engine. It was described as 'The engine for raising water with a power made by fire'

Does James Watt deserve all the credit for the invention of the steam engine?

His features bore the stamp of deep thought ... He was not an early riser and needed ten hours sleep. He took snuff and liked a pipe of tobacco. As a child ... he had shown flair for mathematics and practical work with his hands. He had an observant and well trained mind. Watt was really a boffin ...

B In *James Watt, Instrument Maker*, Rex Wailes describes the character of the inventor

C James Watt and his rotary engine

Steam-power and the use of machinery meant that much more iron and coal were needed. This meant that industries moved to areas where they were most readily available. Steam-powered machines were not just used for spinning and weaving but to produce a range of manufactured goods including wire, nails, chains, cutlery and pottery. Steam-power would also soon provide new, faster and cheaper forms of transport on land and sea. The Industrial Revolution was truly under way.

On Friday last, a steam engine built on Mr Watt's new idea was set up in the presence of a number of scientific gentlemen ... whose hopes were fully satisfied by the excellence of the way it worked.

D A report in the *Birmingham Gazette* from 1776

The idea of using steam to turn a wheel had been thought of many times in history, but only as a toy ... James Watt did not invent the steam engine as is commonly supposed. What he did was to improve it ...

E *Eureka! An Illustrated History of Inventions* (1974), provides another view of James Watt

STEAM POWER PRODUCED MORE GOODS

FACTORIES MOVED TO TOWNS NEAR THE COALFIELDS

FASTER TRAVEL BY RAILWAY

STEAMSHIPS SPEEDED UP FOREIGN TRADE

G Some uses of steam-power

In our towns a great many steam engines of all sizes are working to a great many purposes, such as pumping water, grinding corn, sawing timber, pressing oil from seeds, grinding cutlery ... twisting ropes and cables and making wire.

F An engineer named John Farey wrote this in 1827

1 (a) Look at sources A and C, what are the main differences between the two steam engines?
  (b) Why was James Watt's improvement so important?
  (c) 'Without James Watt, none of the changes referred to in this chapter could have happened.' Do you agree with this statement?

2 If you were allowed to choose just one change that the steam engine brought about, which would you choose as the most important? See if your answer is the same as others in your class. Why are there some differences?

3 How might steam engines have been of benefit in:
  (a) moving goods and passengers on land and sea;
  (b) in the textile industry;
  (c) in mines and ironworks?

4 Once the steam engine was invented, the industrial changes mentioned in this chapter were bound to happen. Do you agree? Give reasons for any answer you give.

5 $\mathcal{W}$ool, cotton and the start of the factory system

Surnames	Dyer, Fuller, Shearer, Weaver
Words	spinster
Phrases	'Dyed in the wool', 'To pull the wool over one's eyes', 'To go for wool and come back shorn'

A Names, words and phrases connected with the woollen industry

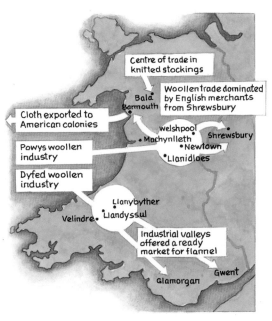

B The Welsh woollen industry

Newtown, Newtown is surely now thy name,

Britannia whole is joyful of thy fame;

... Newtown's new market hall is daily blooming ...

Cambria's masterpiece, manufacturer's pleasure ...

Go on and flourish, thy markets ever bless

With flannel, full of money and success.

For years, the home-based woollen industry had been part of the country's way of life. Rearing sheep and making wool had provided a livelihood for many, and wool merchants had been among the richest in the land. Many everyday words and phrases remind us of the days when wool was so important. (See source A).

By 1838, Newtown was a thriving industrial town with seventy-five mills and a total of 726 **looms**, employing over 3,000 workers. Welsh cloth was hard wearing and popular with industrial workers. It was also used for making army uniforms and prison clothing.

In 1861, the Cambrian Mill was opened by Samuel Owen, whilst an ambitious local draper, Pryce Jones, brought trade to the town by starting a mail order business for Welsh flannels and woollens! It was for good reason that Newtown was called 'the Leeds of Wales'. Llanidloes and Machynlleth were also important textile towns. Although woollens continued to be produced in Dyfed, the Welsh textile industry grew most rapidly in Powys.

Improvements in spinning meant that handloom weavers had as much work as they could handle and did very well indeed. In 1785, Edmund Cartwright invented a power loom. Although it was a poor machine, it was on the right track. Within four years, he had produced a much improved loom driven by a steam engine.

'Smash the looms and save our jobs'

Of course, some did not approve of the new machinery. As the power-operated looms replaced the old fashioned handlooms, so the weavers lost their importance. As their wages fell and their jobs started to disappear, the once well paid weavers and their families became desperately poor. In some areas they rioted and smashed the machinery which was robbing them of their jobs. Known as **Luddites**, they took their name from a strange character called Ned Ludd. (See source D).

The cotton towns

As the population of the country grew, so did the need for more clothing. Although wool was still important, cotton goods were cheaper, easier to wash and healthier. Cotton was to lead the way at the start of the Industrial Revolution.

Lancashire, since it had a suitable climate, lots of skilled workers and the port of Liverpool to receive cargoes of raw cotton from the

C *(left)* **In 1833, the Welsh poet, Robin Ddu Eryri, wrote this poem about Newtown**

United States, became the home of the cotton industry. In that county and neighbouring Yorkshire, Blackburn, Bolton, Preston, Bradford, Halifax, Leeds and Rochdale became important factory towns of the textile industry. Manchester, at the centre of it all, soon earned the nickname 'Cottonopolis'.

(below & right) **Machines which speeded up spinning**

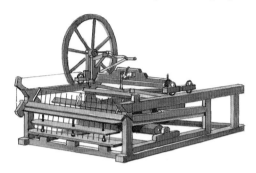

Invented by James Hargreaves in 1763, the Spinning Jenny used a rotating wheel which meant that one person was able to work many spindles at the same time

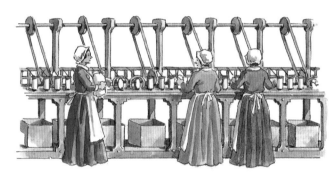

This machine was invented by Richard Arkwright in 1769. Water-powered, it was faster and produced a better yarn than the Spinning Jenny, and was known as the Water Frame

Those who knew the real Ned Ludd could only be amazed by his sudden rise to fame for he was a simple man living in a village ... where he was teased by heartless children. One day, he chased one of the children into a nearby cottage. He lost track of the child but found two knitting frames and took his anger out on them instead. Afterwards in the district, poor Ned was blamed whenever frames were smashed.

D The historian, Christopher Hibbert, wrote this of 'General Ludd' in his book, *The English. A Social History* (1987)

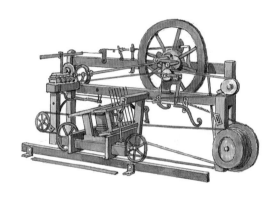

Samuel Crompton combined the ideas of Hargreaves and Arkwright to make the best machine of all. It was known as the Mule

1 (a) Why, at first, did many weavers approve of the new machinery but later came to hate it?
  (b) Make a case for opposing the new textile machinery produced at this time.

2 Using source D and other information in this chapter, say how important you think Ned Ludd was in resisting the changes.

3 Using the information in this chapter and your own ideas, can you work out why the north of England was better for setting up cotton mills than the south?

4 Why did a woollen industry develop in mid-Wales? You may wish to refer to source B and the information in this chapter.

5 Using this chapter and others (e.g. source A in Chapter 1), how well do you think families would be able to adapt to working under these new factory conditions?

6 Arkwright is sometimes called the 'Father of the Factory System.'
  (a) What does this mean?
  (b) Using information in this chapter, do you think this title is fair?

6 New industries – what changes did they bring?

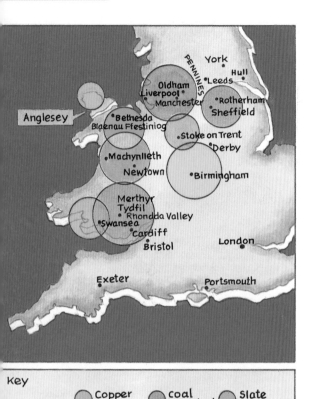

key

Copper · coal iron/steel · Slate · Textiles · Machinery chemicals · Woollens · Pottery

A   The industries of Britain

B   *(below)* The harsh face of the Industrial Revolution - Halifax, a mill town of the nineteenth century

Cotton was not the only industry to do well. The demands of the Industrial Revolution meant that large quantities of iron and coal were needed.

Iron ...

As far as iron was concerned, the old-fashioned ways of **smelting** produced only poor quality cast-iron which was brittle and could not be used to make machinery. In 1784, Henry Cort used iron rods to stir or 'puddle' molten iron to burn off its impurities, and this made it possible to make wrought iron. At the same time, 'puddling' was being used at Merthyr Tydfil by Peter Onions, a foreman working at the Cyfarthfa Ironworks. In South Wales, 'puddling' was known as the 'Welsh method'. The most important iron-producing areas were at Merthyr Tydfil, Ebbw Vale and Blaenavon, in South Wales, and in Yorkshire and the Midlands.

... and coal

The smelting of iron and the development of steam-power meant that more coal was needed. This meant that miners had to dig deeper and tunnel further to reach new, rich seams. The main coalfields were to be found in the South Wales valleys, Durham, Northumberland, Lancashire, Yorkshire, Nottinghamshire, Derbyshire and Staffordshire.

Other industries

In addition to iron and coal, South Wales was also an important area for copper smelting. Copper ore was shipped to Swansea from Anglesey and Cornwall, making Landore and Neath the largest copper-smelting centre in the world. Copper was needed for wire and nails, and was used to cover the bottom ('sheathe') of ships. Lead mined in Dyfed and Clwyd also made Wales one of the richest

lead-producing areas in Britain.

The Midlands, the area around Birmingham, became famous for making machinery and the production of chemicals. Chlorine, soda and sulphuric acid were needed to make bleach and dye, phosphorus to make lucifers (matches) and nitric acid for explosives. For good reason, the region became known as the Black Country.

Pottery was made mainly in Staffordshire. The Potteries, the towns close to Stoke-on-Trent, became famous for china and earthenware products. It was here that Josiah Wedgwood first produced his famous pottery and Thomas Turner made the popular *Willow-pattern* plates.

New industrial towns and cities

All of these changes meant that many people moved from the countryside to the towns to find work. In 1800, the number of people in Wales and England was 9 million and of these only 10 per cent of the people lived in towns. By 1900, the population had risen to over 37 million and 75 per cent of the people were in the towns. The chance to earn good wages in the coalmines and ironworks attracted many workers to South Wales. They came from the Welsh countryside and from further afield, particularly the west of England and Ireland. During the course of the nineteenth century, the population of Wales, just 587,000 in 1801, rose to over 2 million people. (See source C).

Thomas Malthus and his fears

Thomas Malthus, a clergyman living in the south of England, was alarmed at what was happening. He held a very gloomy view of the future. He wrote a book, *Essays on Population*, in which he explained the reason for his fears. Malthus argued that if the population continued to grow at such a rate, a time would come when there would not be enough food and other materials to go around. This, he said, would lead to poverty and cause misery for everyone.

An example of a *Willow-pattern* plate made by Thomas Turner

C Population growth in the towns of Wales and England between 1801 and 1901

	1801	1901
Cardiff	2,000	164,000
Swansea	6,000	95,000
Merthyr Tydfil	8,000	69,000
Newport	1,000	67,000
Wrexham	4,000	15,000
Newtown	1,000	6,500

The population growth of some Welsh towns

Manchester	84,000	866,000
Liverpool	82,000	704,000
Leeds	53,000	429,000
Birmingham	71,000	523,000

The population growth of some English towns

---

1 (a) What clues are given in this chapter as to why particular industries appeared in certain places?
  (b) Draw up a list of the main factors which determine where an industry is likely to be located.

2 Using the information in this and earlier chapters, state why people migrated from the Welsh countryside to the towns.

3 Look at source B.
  (a) Do you think the artist supports or dislikes the new changes? Give reasons for your answer.
  (b) If you wanted to be sure that the artist was accurate, what questions would you want to ask him or her?

4 In the end Thomas Malthus was not right. His ideas though seem reasonable. Can you think what might have happened to disprove his ideas?

7 Life in the factory towns

With so many people looking for work, factory owners were able to hire men cheaply. Afterwards, they showed little interest in the lives of their workers, simply using them to make as much money as they could.

Working conditions

It was quite normal for men to be offered jobs on the condition that their wives and children also worked in the factory. Men worked shifts of up to sixteen hours or more a day. The workers had no holidays and only Sunday was allowed as a day for rest. Levels of wages varied from one industry to another and workers were often paid a **piece rate**, meaning they were paid according to how much they made and not how many hours they worked.

Factories were built to house machines, but without consideration for the comfort of the workers. Factory work was boring and the workers had to endure the endless din made by the machines. Ventilation and lighting were poor and the factories were stifling and damp. Dangerous machinery was left unguarded and this led to terrible accidents. For many years, the government made no attempt to look into working conditions. Owners were left to run their factories and treat their workers much as they liked.

Children in the factories

Children were expected to work from the age of five and some even younger. They did simple minding and cleaning jobs which meant they often had to crawl under the machines. If they were tired and fell asleep, they were likely to be strapped by their **overseer**. Their parents dared not complain in case they lost their own jobs! Women and children received lower wages than men.

That from and after this Date, One Months' Notice will be given and required, and subject to the following RULES AND REGULATIONS:—

If any Workman absents himself from his Work (unless in case of Illness or by Permission of the Agent or Foreman of his department), a Deduction will be made from his Wages as follows:—

FINERS.—For every Turn lost, 1d. per Ton upon the Iron made by them during the Week.

PUDDLERS.—For every Turn, 3d. per Ton on the Iron made by them in each Week.

HEATERS.—For every Turn, 1d. per Ton on the Iron made by them in each Week.

From every description of Workmen, for the Loss of One Turn, 1s. in the Pound upon their Week's Earnings.

From every Man who leaves his Work during his Turn (without Permission), 2s. 6d. in the Pound upon his Week's Earnings.

For Dowlais Iron Co.,
JOHN EVANS.

Dowlais Iron Works, 12th May, 1853.

M. W. WHITE, PRINTER AND BOOKSELLER, MERTHYR-TYDFIL.

A A notice relating to conditions in a factory

B A contemporary artist's impression of the inside of a cotton factory

The plight of the orphan apprentices

The state of the poor orphans was most sad. Without parents to care for them, they were placed in the care of the **parish** and sent to work as **apprentices** for local factory owners. They were supposed to be taught a trade but were often ill-treated and used only as cheap labour. They lived in lodging houses, received little or no payment apart from their keep and seldom had enough to eat. It was not surprising that some ran away.

Apprentice Absconded.

RUN AWAY, from Cromford Cotton Mills, in the County of Derby; JOHN FLINT, by Trade a Joiner; he is a ſtout young Man, about 20 Years of Age, Red Hair, and has a Mole on his Face.
Whoever will give Information to Mr. RICHARD ARKWRIGHT, of Cromford aforeſaid, of the Perſon that Employs the above Apprentice, ſhall be handſomely rewarded for their Trouble.

C 'Apprentice Absconded'. An advertisement in the *Derby Mercury* asks for information about a runaway apprentice

The accidents which occur are very severe and numerous ... Many are the result of the want of fencing to the machinery ... The shawls of females, or their long hair and the loose sleeves of the boys are frequent causes of dreadful **mutilation**.

D A Parliamentary Report of 1842

Rising before the break of day ... During the day, they are ... continually engaged in a crowded room at a high temperature ... when finally dismissed for the day, they are exhausted in body and mind.

E Peter Gaskell described the average day in a book about factory life, written in 1833

F (left) A cartoon drawn by Robert Cruickshank in 1832

1 Look at sources B and F.
   (a) Are there any similarities?
   (b) What is different?
   (c) Because source B is more lifelike, it must be more accurate than source F. Do you agree?
   (d) Is there any evidence elsewhere in this chapter which does not support what is shown in these sources?

2 Look at source C. Why do you think Richard Arkwright was so keen to get back the runaway apprentice?

3 Using your own knowledge and the information in this chapter, outline what working conditions of that time would not be allowed today.

milk   1p a pint
flour 1p a lb
sugar 4p a lb
butter 9p a lb
meat   2-4p a lb
tea   4p a lb
eggs   1p for 3
potatoes ½p a lb

A The prices of goods in the mid-1800s

1 lb is equivalent to 0.454 kilograms

1 pint is equivalent to 0.568 litres

B A token worth a shilling (5p) and 'payable in goods', used by the Penydarren Ironworks at Merthyr Tydfil

Wages, prices and housing

For all workers, discipline was very strict. Fines had to be paid by those who broke the rules by arriving late, falling asleep, being careless or just talking to someone. There was always a foreman on hand to check that work was done properly and the rules were obeyed. A factory worker interviewed in 1834 said that he earned £1.02p for working 72 hours a week. His wife received 45p and his daughter 20p. Of course, if workers were away from work because of sickness, they received no pay at all! See source A to find out what their wages would have bought.

The tommy shops

It was not unusual for factory owners to run their own shops - **tommy shops** as the workers called them. To make sure that their men spent at least some of their money in the factory owner's shops, wages were partly paid in tokens which could only be used in them to buy goods. Prices were high and the quality of the goods so poor, that workers spoke of 'tommy rot'. This unfair practice was known as the **truck system.**

The condition of workers' homes

Workmen depended on their masters not only for their pay, but also for their homes. Around their factories the owners built rows of closely packed, back-to-back houses. The smallest houses had one room up and one down. Slate-roofed and stone-walled, they were seldom built to any plan but gradually grew into a warren of streets. The workers paid rent for their homes and this was taken from their wages. In order to make a little extra money, some families took in lodgers and this made the problem of over-crowding even worse.

C *(right)* The type of housing built for workers in the factory towns

Homes had no lavatories but shared earth closets in the alleyways at the back of the houses. Water had to be fetched from taps in the streets. The poorest workers had no real homes but found shelter in lean-to shacks. The people made what they could of their lice-ridden, unventilated dwellings. With the water pipe liable to come into contact with untreated sewage there was always the risk of **epidemics** of **dysentery** and **cholera**.

The room was in a horrible state ... excrement all over and the place reeking with filth. The beds were black and shining with body sweat ... I swept maggots away from under the bed ...

D In 1852, the *Bath Chronicle* carried a description of a house

... there are pits: water gathers in those pits into which there have been thrown dead dogs and cats ... The water is still used for culinary [cooking] purposes.

E An extract from Parliamentary Papers of 1849

F The centres of many towns and cities became dreadfully overcrowded. This is a contemporary artist's impression of Cardiff in the mid-nineteenth century

1 (a) Today people would not put up with these dreadful working conditions. Why did they not cause much trouble during this period?

(b) 'The changes were mainly better for women and children than for men.' Is there any evidence in this chapter that supports this view?

(c) Why do you think the government did little to improve the condition of working people?

2 If you had been in charge of the income of a factory family, how would you have spent the week's wages? Produce a list and use it to work out the kind of meals the family might have had.

3 Were the houses now being built, much more unhealthy than those of an earlier time? You may find source C in this chapter, and sources B and C in Chapter 2, helpful.

> Mr Anthony Hill is a gentleman. Mr Bailey has a low born, purse-string cunning. Mr Crawshay is beyond all rule and description and impossible to account for.

A In a diary, Lady Charlotte Guest made notes about the town's ironmasters

B Penry Williams's painting of the inside of the Cyfarthfa Ironworks

> A puddler received £1.75 a week and a shingler, £2. The sales agent earned £1,000 a year and the works manager, £750. That year, the works made a profit of £59,038!

C (above) The book, *Merthyr Historian*, provides details of wages at the Dowlais Works in 1845

Merthyr Tydfil - the furnacemen's town

Merthyr Tydfil began to develop during the early years of the Industrial Revolution. By 1851, the population had risen to 46,000 and it was by far the biggest town in Wales.

Ironworks and ironmasters

The town grew around a number of great ironworks. There was the Dowlais Works started by Thomas Lewis of Llanishen and managed by John Guest, the Plymouth Works of Anthony Bacon, the Penydarren Works set up by Francis Homfray and the Cyfarthfa Works, run by generations of the colourful Crawshay family. The founder was Richard Crawshay, a hard but fair employer. He was followed by his son and then his grandson, both called William. The second William built himself a splendid home, Cyfarthfa Castle, but, as we shall see, had to deal with serious riots in the town. Then came his son, Robert Thompson Crawshay, a fiery and obstinate man, who didn't get on with his workers or his own family! Dowlais Ironworks became the biggest in the world. By 1845, it employed 7,300 men, women and children, and its eighteen furnaces produced 89,000 tonnes of iron each year.

Working at the furnaces

Making iron required the skills of many different workers. Puddlers stirred the molten iron, shinglers hammered it and the catchers fed the iron bars through rollers. As in the mines, the employment of children was normal. In 1866, the Dowlais Works employed 669 boys and girls aged between ten and thirteen. Pull-up boys raised the furnace door by tugging at a chain, and boys and girls dragged wagons full of cinders to the tips around the town.

When iron was wanted, the pay of furnacemen was good but when demand fell, the ironmasters were quick to cut wages. Working in the heat of the furnaces was uncomfortable and dangerous. Molten metal which splashed from the moulds onto the workmen caused terrible scars and could burn flesh through to the bone.

D (below) Merthyr Tydfil in 1830. Behind the ironworks and the workers' houses can be seen the home of the Crawshay family - the magnificent Cyfarthfa Castle

The town and its people

The chance of work drew many to the town. They came mainly from the Welsh countryside, England and Ireland. By 1862, there were 10,634 houses in Merthyr.

The workers' homes were small and in some areas there was no sanitation at all. Overcrowding was a big problem. Sometimes families had to share houses and most homes took in a lodger. The worst slum area was the maze of back-to-back hovels known as 'China'.

In 1849, there was an outbreak of cholera in the town which claimed the lives of 1,382 people. There was another outbreak of cholera in 1866. When times were bad, people took their belongings to a **pawnshop**. If they ran into debt, they were likely to have their furniture and goods taken away by the **Court of Requests.** As in other areas, there were company shops which accepted tokens and sold shoddy goods at high prices. The Crawshays never used the truck system and boasted that they always 'paid for hard work in hard money'. Lady Charlotte Guest, wife of the owner of the Dowlais Works, took an interest in the welfare of people and in the state of local schools and workhouses.

The boom in iron lasted until midway through the nineteenth century. Then, when production changed to steel (and iron-ore had to be imported from abroad), the Welsh industry moved from Merthyr to better sites on the coast at Port Talbot, Briton Ferry, Aberavon, Neath and Swansea. The industry lingered on at Merthyr for a number of years but the great days were over.

All the hills around the town have a scorched and blackened look … The houses are in general low and mean … Merthyr, however, can show several remarkable buildings though of gloomy, horrid, Satanic character.

E In 1854, George Borrow set out to travel around Wales. In his book, *Wild Wales*, he describes Merthyr Tydfil

Dic went through the arch and into China. The alleys were crowded with the workers from Ynys and Cyfarthfa. Wizened faces too old to die stared down from cracked windows as he passed, half-starved children, the waste of iron, stared up from crowded doorsteps. A beggar jeered at him, waved his stumps, Dai No Arms who wouldn't go through the rollers.

F 'China' is mentioned in Alexander Cordell's novel, *The Fire People*

G A group of Merthyr ironworkers

---

1 (a) **How far does source B support the paragraphs describing the ironworks?**
   (b) **What evidence is there to suggest that the industrial changes brought benefits to some workers?**

2 **There are several clues in this chapter which indicate that living conditions in workers' houses were unpleasant. Use these clues to write a paragraph about living conditions in Merthyr Tydfil.**

3 (a) **Do you think source D accurately shows what it was like to live in Merthyr Tydfil in 1830? Give reasons for your answer.**
   (b) **'Source F is a story whereas source G is a photograph. This means that we can rely on the photograph but not the story.' Do you agree?**

4 **Do you think that the working conditions of children at this time were better in a textile mill or an ironworks? Use information from these sources and others (for example, source B on page 18). Give reasons for your decision.**

8 *W*elsh coal

There are two coalfields in Wales. The largest and most important is in South Wales and stretches across much of mid-Glamorgan and Gwent. There is a smaller coalfield in North Wales.

The South Wales coalfield

The demand for coal

Coal was first taken from outcrops on hillsides where it was close to the surface. Then shafts were dug into the ground and coal removed from around the bottom of the pit. Because of their shape these were known as 'bell-pits'. Needed for smelting, driving machinery and, soon, to power locomotives and ships, the demand for coal grew rapidly. As mining became big business, so pits were sunk and men sent underground to tunnel further and further into the seams. Welsh coal was much sought after and was sent to London to be exported abroad.

Among the famous Welsh coal owners were Thomas Powell, John Nixon and Walter Coffin. David Davies, who came from Llandinam, set up the Ocean Company in the Rhondda. Coal was the fuel of the Industrial Revolution and it became so important that people spoke of 'King Coal'.

Getting the coal

The most common method of mining coal was the 'pillar and stall' system. Miners removed coal from working areas known as stalls, but left pillars of coal behind to support the roof. The result was a honeycomb effect and the system was wasteful. Gradually it was replaced by 'longwalling'. Now the miners worked on a wide front and, as they advanced, used props to support the roof. When the props were removed, the space was filled with rubble.

Explosives were used for blasting but hewers worked at the coal-face with picks and shovels. Mining was dangerous and, as the miners went deeper and tunnelled further from the pithead to reach new and richer seams, so the risks increased. Mines were liable to flood and there was always the risk of rock-falls and explosions. Ventilation was needed to get rid of the stale air and gases, which the miners called **'choke-damp'** and **'fire-damp'**. The use of fires to create a draught was dangerous and gave way to a system of doors which were used to control the flow of air. Even though a single spark could cause an explosion, miners used naked candles to provide light. The invention of a safety lamp by Sir Humphry Davy in 1815 greatly reduced this risk. The lamp gave off only a glimmer of light but showed if gas was present. The waste from the pits was taken to nearby mountainsides to form unsightly tips.

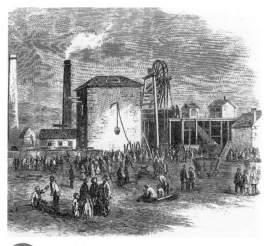

A An artist's impression of the colliery at Port Talbot which was sunk in 1847

B This picture gives some ideas of working conditions underground (1910)

Children in the mines

Until laws were passed to prevent it, women and children were employed in the mines. In 1841, of the 45,000 people employed in South Wales pits, 10,000 were under 18 years of age and 3,000 under 13 years. Very young boys and girls aged no more than five or six were used as doorkeepers or 'trappers', whilst older children worked as 'trammers'. Chained to trams laden with coal, they pulled the heavy loads along a maze of narrow tunnels.

In 1854, the output of the South Wales coalfield was over 8 million tonnes. It rose rapidly. And yet, coal's best years were still to come! The figures below show the growth in output.

1854	8,636,000 tonnes
1875	14,400,000 tonnes
1885	24,733,000 tonnes
1895	33,570,000 tonnes
1900	39,959,000 tonnes

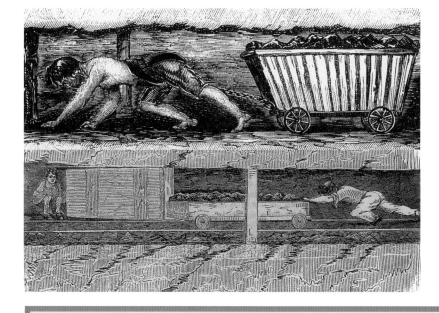

Year	Place	Killed
1855	Cymmer	114
1860	Risca	145
1867	Ferndale	178
1878	Abercarn	268
1880	Risca	119
1890	Llanerch	176
1890	Park Slip	116
1894	Cilfynydd	290
1905	Wattstown	119
1913	Senghenydd	439

C Some Welsh colliery disasters in which over a hundred miners lost their lives

I am a haulier ... I have been at work five years, I first kept a door. I start work at six and work for twelve hours every day. I get eleven shillings [55p] a week ...

D In 1842, a girl aged 13 gave this account of her everyday work, to a mines' inspector

E (left) Pictures from a government report of 1842 show the type of work done by children in the mines

---

1. What information do you need before you can state confidently whether source E is accurate or not?

2. What clues are given in this chapter as to the health risks of people who worked in coal mines in Wales?

3. Can you suggest reasons why the coal industry was more important in South Wales than North Wales - apart from the amount of coal available?

4. (a) What changes might an old person, alive in 1900, have noticed as he or she grew up in the South Wales coalfield?
   (b) Which changes might they have regarded as being the most important?

5. Having looked at several industries, how important do you think that children were in making the industrial changes succeed? Give reasons for your answer.

A A coal-mining community. The colliery and rows of miners' terraced houses at Blaengarw can be seen

B A collier fills his tram with coal

Meeting a cross-eyed woman or a rag and bone man was said to bring bad luck. Some thought the sight of a magpie or robin was a bad omen and would turn back if they saw any of these on the way to work.

C Some miners were very superstitious

Miners and their families

The life of a miner and his family was harsh. The sharing of hardship meant that families living around the pits formed closely-knit communities and were always willing to help each other.

Working down the pit

Once underground, miners worked in pairs and each miner had his **'butty'**. Colliers were paid according to the amount of coal they produced and they had to cut coal in the largest pieces possible. Men could be fined for 'breaking lumps unnecessarily'.

They ate their meals at the coal-face, when bread and cheese was swilled down with cold tea. Miners received quantities of free coal for their own use. Not all miners worked at the coal-face, some were roadmen, hauliers or repairers, and ostlers were needed to look after the pit ponies. There were also those who worked above the ground, like blacksmiths and the men who sorted and weighed the coal. Miners often had amusing nicknames - Twm Wasgod Bert (Twm Pretty Waistcoat), Bob Un Glust (Bob One Ear), Wil Un Fagal (Will One Crutch) and John Tatws Raw (John Raw Potatoes).

Mining - a family tradition

For most boys, there was little chance of getting away from the colliery. Mining became a family tradition and sons just assumed they would follow their fathers down the pit. Boys even looked forward to the time when they could go to work with their fathers and uncles, and begin to earn money.

A coal-miner's life

A hooter sounded to mark the beginning and end of each shift and a series of short blasts meant there had been an accident. Miners could be crippled by injury, and sometimes suffered from **pneumoconiosis**. This was caused by breathing in air full of coal dust. Some employers were more considerate than others. Durham-born John Nixon, who owned mines in the Cynon Valley, and David Davies, were better than most. Some contributed to the building of workmen's halls, libraries and institutes.

David Davies, Llandinam

David Davies was a man from a humble background. One of eleven children, he left school at the age of eleven, and worked as a sawyer, becoming known as Davies 'Top Sawyer'. A man of strong build and energy, Davies saved enough money to go into business. He was involved in the building of railways and owned coal-mines in the Rhondda Valley. Davies became very wealthy and was elected Member of Parliament for Cardigan. He was a deeply religious man who gave generously to good causes.

Since miners' pay depended on the price of coal, they were best off in years when coal was in great demand. Miners stood up to unfair employers, yet were wary of those who showed them kindness.

Home life

Since everything depended on it, the mine was the centre of family and community life. Miners and their families lived close to the pit in rows of terraced houses. Managers and officials had larger homes than ordinary miners. Houses were built to provide for only the barest needs; rooms to live and sleep in and a fireplace for cooking and heating. Furniture was simple - a table, chairs, some cupboards and a bedstead. With no pit-head baths, colliers went home black with coal dust and washed in zinc tubs filled with water heated on the kitchen fire.

The miner's wife, 'mam' to her children, was always busy cooking, tidying her home and making, repairing and washing clothes. In addition to her own family, she often had a lodger to look after as well.

On Sundays, many families put on their best clothes and went to chapel. Men wore suits with waistcoats, nailed boots and caps or bowler hats. Women dressed in long skirts, high-necked blouses and hats decorated with flowers.

E A miner washes as best he can in front of the kitchen fire

He asked no man to do a job which he was not willing to do … They seldom grumbled and men were heard to say that they would rather work for David Davies for a shilling a day less than for other employers.

D In his book *David Davies - Topsawyer*, Peter Lewis explained how Davies got on with his workmen

I was in lodgings … there were six or seven other miners lodging there. It was only a house with three bedrooms so … we were sleeping on a rota basis. I'd gallop home to be first to have a bath.

F A miner's account of his daily routine from *Coalface*, by Richard Keen

---

1 (a) Why do you think that mine owners did not want workers to break coal up into small bits?
  (b) Why do you think the mining communities were so closely knit?

2 Look at source C. Because it is only about a superstition, this source tells us nothing useful about mining life. Do you agree?

3 In what ways do sources E and F back up what is mentioned elsewhere in this chapter about home life?

4 Of the different industries you have looked at so far, which do you feel was the most dangerous for:
  (a) men;
  (b) women;
  (c) children?
  Give reasons for your answer.

5 Piece together the evidence in this chapter to produce an account of a typcial day's work as a miner in the nineteenth century. Try to express what their opinions and feelings may have been at the type of work they did, their living conditions and the general environment around them.

9 Welsh slate

As the mining of coal and making of iron became important in South Wales, slate quarrying was the main industry in North Wales. Slate is rock formed in such a way that it can be easily split into sheets.

One of the largest slate quarries was owned by Richard Pennant. The son of a Liverpool merchant who had made a fortune from his sugar plantations in Jamaica, Pennant married the heiress to part of the Penrhyn estate in Snowdonia. He bought out the quarry owners in the area and then opened his own quarry at Bethesda. Others began quarries at Ffestiniog and Llanberis. Bethesda and other quarrymens' villages such as Ebenezer, Herbron and Salem, took their names from their chapels.

The reason that slate was so important was that it was needed to roof the houses in the new industrial towns of England and Wales. Yet it had other uses. Slate could be used as paving slabs for floors, as walls, and could be written on in chalk by children learning to write. Schools supplied children with 'slates' which, once used, could be wiped clean.

Quarrying and cutting slate

Slate could be cut directly from the side of a mountain or it could be mined from seams beneath the ground. Quarrying was dangerous. Explosives had to be put in place by rockmen on ladders or hanging on ropes from the roof. Once the slate had been removed, great caverns were left behind. Like coal and iron, quarrying slate produced waste which was piled on the hills around. Quarrymen worked in teams. Each team was made up of 'rockmen' who first removed the blocks of slate, a 'splitter' who split it into narrow sheets and a 'dresser' who cut it to size. Since roofing slate had to be less than half a centimetre thick, splitting was a very skilled job but dressing could be done by an apprentice.

It was the custom for the quarry manager to agree a 'bargain' with the team leader. The men were then given a section of the rockface on which to work. The team was paid according to the number of slates it produced and so it was important that the splitter did not spoil too many!

Once they were ready, the slates were taken by pack-horse down the dangerous mountain roads to the coast at Bangor and Caernarvon. Richard Pennant, now Lord Penrhyn, built a railway to connect his quarries with his own harbour at Port Penrhyn. Welsh-born William Madocks was responsible for Portmadoc which became very important in the export of slate. North Wales slate was thought to be the best and was much sought after the world over. Lord Penrhyn's quarries produced nearly 12,000 slates a year and

A The slate quarry at Bethesda

B A splittter at work. The wages of his team depended on his skill made him a very rich man.

Men working at the quarry breathed in dust so that many suffered from **silicosis**. In 1850, in return for their hard work and the risks taken, quarrymen were paid just 12p a day! The social life of the quarrymen was centred around the 'Caban'. This was a type of canteen where men were able to meet, discuss matters and arrange entertainment.

Relations between quarrymen and their masters were not good. Hard work for low wages, and the fact that the quarry owners were English and their workers Welsh, led to bad feeling. In 1874, the North Wales Quarryman's Union was formed. Lord Penrhyn was against the Union and sacked their leaders. Between 1896 and 1903 there were strikes and lock-outs. During the Penrhyn dispute, the few quarrymen who sided with the owner had to be escorted to work by policemen and soldiers. Those who backed the Union put notices up in the windows of their homes - Nid oes bradwr yn y ty hwn ('There is no traitor in this house'). The strike helped to ruin the industry which already faced other serious problems. Cheaper slate was being brought from abroad and people were beginning to use tiles, instead of slates, to roof their houses.

I believe the disease is due to the way quarrymen prepare their tea. They send a boy to a house ... given by the owners for their workers' comfort ... to prepare the tea with tea, sugar and water in the same kettle. It stews before the men drink it. That habit, in my opinion, is the cause of the problem ...

C A Blaenau Ffestiniog doctor's evidence to an enquiry looking into the causes of silicosis. This was taken from *The North Wales Quarrymen,* by R Merfyn Jones (1981)

... the Caban was more than a place to eat, it was a special sort of club. It was a centre for discussion ... subjects included education, politics, religion and advice for those about to be married. The Caban was the centre of social life and each organised its own eisteddfod.

D From *Candles to Caplamps,* by J G Isherwood

E *(left)* Portmadoc with masses of slates waiting on the quayside. The photograph was taken in 1896

1 (a) Look at source C. The doctor is quite clearly wrong and so the source tells us nothing useful. Do you agree?
  (b) Look at source E. In what ways might a historian of the Welsh slate industry find this useful?

2 Slate has been in the area for millions of years. Why then did the industry really only develop after the late eighteenth century? You should try to come up with more than one possible reason.

3 What similarities and differences can you find between the way quarrymen responded to their conditions and those in the other industries you have studied?

4 Of the industries studied, which do you think has made the greatest difference to:
  (a) the people who lived in industrial areas;
  (b) the landscape?
  Give reasons for your answer.

IO $\mathcal{P}$opular protest

A A cartoon of 1819 shows men, women and children being cut down during the Peterloo Massacre

The meeting was a tremendous one ... a noise ... I saw a party of cavalry in blue and white uniform, come trotting sword in hand ... they dashed forward ... and their sabres were plied to hew a way through held-up hands and defenceless heads ...

B In *Passages in the Life of a Radical* (1844), Samuel Bamford recalled the protest at St Peter's Fields

As we have seen, weavers in the Midlands smashed the machines which were robbing them of their work. The Luddites were not the only people to suffer hardship and so turn to violence.

In 1815, the war against Napoleon came to an end and thousands of soldiers came home to search for work. They joined the farm hands who had lost their jobs in the countryside and came to the towns. For those with work, wages were low and life in the new factory towns was hard. Workers tried to join forces and make their masters pay better wages. This scared the factory owners who urged the government to pass laws to stop their workers combining together. The laws were known as the **Combination Acts**. Another cause of hardship was the Corn Laws. These were passed to make sure the profits of farmers were not affected by importing cheap cereals from abroad. This meant that bread was expensive and beyond the means of families struggling to live on low wages.

The government took no action to help people and just allowed them to cope as best they could. Such a policy of non-interference is called *laissez faire*. With the French Revolution still fresh in their minds, the government used informers and spies to keep an eye on the people. They were particularly worried by the activities of the radicals who urged people to take action and become more **militant**. William Cobbett, self-educated and the son of a farm worker, produced a popular weekly pamphlet, the *Political Register*. In it, he drew the people's attention to the many injustices which affected their daily lives. Without the right to vote, they could not influence Parliament so they had to find other means of drawing attention to their complaints.

In 1816, there were riots at Spa Fields in London when a speaker, Henry Hunt, called for changes in the system of government. The following year, a large number of spinners from the mill towns planned to march to London to deliver a petition. They carried blankets for use at night and the event was called the March of the Blanketeers. They were harassed by soldiers, and of the 600 who set out, only one reached London. This was followed by a large demonstration in Manchester.

The Peterloo Massacre

In 1819, some 80,000 people assembled to demonstrate at St Peter's Fields in Manchester. They were to be addressed by Henry Hunt. The meeting was orderly but the authorities were frightened by the number present and ordered soldiers to disperse the crowd.

The men, mounted on horseback, drew their swords and charged into the mass of people. Eleven civilians were killed and some 500 wounded. In mockery of the famous Battle of Waterloo, the event became known as the Peterloo Massacre.

Six months later, Arthur Thistlewood and a group of extremists tried to murder members of the government, whilst they were at dinner in Grosvenor Square. They were arrested in Cato Street. When sentenced to death, Thistlewood seemed unconcerned and merely took a pinch of **snuff**. Later, he was hanged and beheaded.

The government responded by taking harsh measures against the people. The Habeas Corpus Act, which ensures that people cannot be held for long periods without being brought to trial, was scrapped for a time.

Six Acts were passed which banned public meetings and allowed private houses to be searched. A tax was put on pamphlets and people found guilty of writing against the government ran the risk of being **transported.** For good reason, the laws were nicknamed the 'Gag Acts'.

For a while there was peace but when the unrest did start again, Wales was to be in the thick of it.

Whereas printed pamphlets ... tending to excite hatred of the Government have lately been published in great numbers and at very small prices ... all pamphlets for sale for less than the sum of sixpence shall pay the same tax as newspapers.

C One of the Six Acts

And now, Twopenny Trash go your way ... Ten thousand wagon loads of books ... have never caused a millionth part of the trouble that you have caused. [Adapted].

D From a copy of the *Political Register,* by William Cobbett

E *(left)* A cartoon from 1819 by George Cruikshank. It shows members of the government fleeing in panic before a monster representing the French Revolution. The monster is in the shape of a guillotine and is wearing the hat of a French revolutionary.

1 (a) Look at source A. What impression do you think the artist is trying to give?
  (b) Do you feel that source B agrees or disagrees with the image of source A? Give reasons for your answer.

2 What does source E tell us about what people believed at the time?

3 Look at source D. What point do you think William Cobbett is trying to make?

4 (a) If the government were so worried about the poorer people causing trouble, why did they not try to help them more?
  (b) 'The working people and their supporters saw no alternative but violence to get things improved.' Do you feel that the information in this chapter agrees with this view or not?

Dic Penderyn – Welsh folk hero?

A A local artist's impression of nineteenth-century Merthyr Tydfil

The alternative is violence, and we do not seek violence although our cause is just. It is a time of depressed trade and our wages are cut. But were our wages raised by Crawshay when times were good?

B In Alexander Cordell's novel, *The Fire People*, one of the characters addresses the meeting at Waun Hill

These riots, as alarming as they are mischievous ... were caused by alleged low wages. At the start, a strike amongst workmen, the alarming way in which they assembled and the threats they made gave good cause for concern that there would be violence.

C The *Newgate Calendar* carried a report of the events

The ironworkers of Merthyr Tydfil had many reasons to be dissatisfied. During the early 1830s there was excitement in the town as men campaigned for the vote to be given to more people. In the spring of 1831, the iron industry was badly affected by a **slump**. William Crawshay, an important local ironmaster, threatened to cut the wages of his workers.

There was anger and as tension increased, a meeting was arranged on nearby Waun Hill. At the meeting, speakers stirred up an excitable crowd. Afterwards, a crowd went to the town and ransacked the Court of Requests. Lewis Lewis known locally as Lewsyn Yr Heliwr (Lewis the Huntsman), was among the leaders of the mob.

The ironmasters were scared and sent for help. Soon afterwards, a regiment of Scottish soldiers arrived from Brecon. Events came to a head on Friday 3 June. As the ironmasters met the workers' leaders inside the Castle Inn, workers and troops stood toe to toe outside. There was a scuffle and the soldiers opened fire. As a result, twenty civilians were killed and a soldier was stabbed in the thigh.

The situation seemed to be getting out of hand, so more soldiers were sent for. Once again the workers gathered on the Waun but this time John Guest, an ironmaster and magistrate, was present together with 400 soldiers. He read the **Riot Act** and then the troops moved forward with their bayonets fixed. The crowd gave way and broke up. The Merthyr riots were as good as over.

The ring leaders were rounded up and then brought to trial in Cardiff. Three men were sentenced to transportation for life and two sentenced to death - Lewis Lewis and Richard Lewis. Richard Lewis, known as Dic Penderyn, was found guilty of wounding the soldier.

The sentence on Lewis Lewis was reduced to transportation but, in spite of requests for a reprieve, Richard Lewis was hanged in Cardiff on 13 August 1831. Aged only 23, he protested his innocence to the end. After his execution, he became a working-class hero and a great deal of **folklore** grew up about him. To confuse the matter further, 45 years later a Welshman who had emigrated to the United States and who was close to death, confessed to the crime for which Richard Lewis had been hanged! After 1831, Merthyr Tydfil was never quite the same and tension continued in the town.

I saw a soldier coming up the steps, I saw him struggle to keep his musket which he lost ... as he was on the top step, Richard Lewis charged him with a bayonet and wounded him in the thigh.

D At the trial, this evidence was given by James Abbott, a local hairdresser

I am going to suffer unjustly. God, who knows all things, knows it is so.

G On 20 August 1831, *The Cambrian* newspaper reported the last words of Dic Penderyn

I was wounded in the right hip. I don't know the man that wounded me. I saw both prisoners in the crowd, I did not see them laying hands on anyone.

E The soldier, Donald Black, also gave evidence

Glamorganshire Summer Assize, July 9, 1831.
SENTENCES OF THE PRISONERS,
TRIED BEFORE
THE HONOURABLE MR. JUSTICE BOSANQUET.

1 *David Morgan*, aged 19, *Labourer*—Feloniously and violently assaulting (with intent to ravish and carnally know) Mary Thomas, of Roath.—*Two years imprisonment.*
2 *Francis Jones*, 37, *Labourer*—3 *William Williams*, 39, *Cordwainer*—Stealing one drawing knife and other articles, the property of Rees Jones and William Jones, of Merthyr Tidvil. Also stealing one sack, and one brass pan, the property of Daniel Jenkin and Rees Jenkin, of Brecon.—*Six months each.*
4 *Henry Lewis alias Matthews*, 23, *Boatman*—Breaking into the warehouse of Lewis Williams, of Cardiff, and stealing therefrom a quantity of wine and other articles.—*Transported for life.*
5 *Thomas Rowland*, 37, *Mason*—Breaking into the dwelling-house of Thomas Harry, of Cardiff, and stealing therein one hat and one bonnet.—*Death recorded.*
6 *William John*, 27, *Labourer*—Knowingly and wilfully sending a letter to the Honorable W. B. Grey, without any name, threatening to destroy the house of the said W. B. Grey.—*Seven years transportation.*
7 *Catherine Gwin*, 30, *wife of William Gwin*—Wilful murder of her male child, at Pontcanna.—*To be confined during his Majesty's pleasure.*
8 *Catherine Badger*, 40, *Spinster*—9 *Thomas Gibbs*, 60, *Farmer*—Wilful murder of a female child.—*C. Badger one year's imprisonment, and T. Gibbs acquitted.*
10 *William Williams*, 32, *Puddler*—Burglariously breaking into the dwelling-house of John Greenhouse, of Merthyr, and stealing therein one pair of boots and other articles.—*Death recorded.*
11 *John Phelps*, 44, *Cordwainer*—With menaces and by force, demanding of and from Jane Williams, one Bible, and divers pictures, of Thomas Williams, of Merthyr, with intent to steal the same.—*Fourteen years transportation.*
12 *Lewis Lewis*, 37, *Miner*—With divers others, riotously assembling, and destroying in part the dwelling-house, and burning and destroying the fixtures, books, furniture, &c. in the dwelling-house of Joseph Coffin, at Merthyr.—*Death.*
13 *Thomas Kinsey*, 25, *Labourer*—Riotously assembling at Coedycymmer, in the county of Brecon, and at Merthyr Tidvil, and robbing E. Kins, Esq. Surgeon of the 93d Regiment of Highlanders, of his sword.—*Acquitted.*
14 *Richard Lewis*, 23, *Miner*—Riotously assembling, with others, at Merthyr Tidvil, and feloniously attacking and wounding Daniel Black, of the 93d Regiment, with a bayonet, whilst he was on duty.—*Death.*
15 *Thomas Rowland*, 22, *Puddler*—Riotously assembling with divers others at Merthyr Tidvil, and attacking John Barr, a Private of the 93rd Regiment, and disarming him of his musket.—*Acquitted.*
16 *William Williams*, 32, *Puddler*—Unlawfully assembling, with divers others, at Merthyr Tidvil, with force and arms, and carrying a red flag before such persons.—*Acquitted.*
17 *Thomas Vaughan*, 21, *Miner*—Forcing his way with divers others, into the house of Thomas Lewis, of Merthyr Tidvil, and violently assaulting him, and by threats compelling him to part with his property.—*Death recorded.*
18 *Thomas David*, 23, *Collier*—Riotously assembling, with divers others, and demanding one canister of powder of Benjamin Lewis, of Aberdare, and with having presented a loaded gun a Stephen Harry, of Merthyr.—*Acquitted.*

F A list of the prisoners tried and sentenced at Glamorgan Summer Assize in 1831

H A modern artist's impression of the hanging of Dic Penderyn (1986)

---

1 Look at sources B and C.
   (a) What point do you think the character in source B is trying to make?
   (b) Is source C sympathetic to the workers in Merthyr Tydfil? What is your evidence for this?

2 What verdict do you think the jury should have come up with in the trial of Dic Penderyn? Does your view agree with others in the class?

3 Look at source F. What does this source suggest about:
   (a) the types of crime;
   (b) the criminals;
   (c) the amount of crime;
   (d) attitudes towards particular types of crime?

4 Dic Penderyn was hanged as a criminal. Why then, do you think that he became a working-class hero after his death?

Rebecca and the toll–gates

ABERYSTWITH SOUTH GATES
(CLEAR) ABERYSTWITH NORTH GATES.

Rate of Toll to be taken at this Gate.

For every Horse or other Beast drawing any Coach, Chariot, £-s-d
Berlin, Landau, Landaulet, Barouche, Chaise, Phaeton,
Vis-a-Vis, Calash, Curricle, Car, Chair, Gig, Hearse, Caravan
Litter, or any such like Carriage — — — — 0-0-6
For every Horse or other Beast, except Asses drawing
any Waggon, Wain, Cart, or other such like Carriage — 0-0-4
For every Ass drawing any Cart, Carriage, or other Vehicle – 0-0-2
For every Horse or Mule, laden or unladen, and not drawing – 0-0-1½
For every Ass, laden or unladen and not drawing — — 0-0-½
For every Horse or other Animal employed in carrying, drawing,
or conveying any lime to be used for the purpose of manure – 0-0-2
For every drove of Oxen, Cows, or Neat Cattle, the sum of Ten Pence
per Score, and so in proportion for any greater or less number
For every drove of Calves, Hogs, Sheeps, or Lambs, the sum of Five
Pence per Score, and so in proportion for any greater or less number.

EXEMPTION FROM TOLLS

Horses or Carriages attending her Majesty, or any of the Royal Family, or
returning therefrom; Horses or Carriages employed for the repairs of any
Turnpike Roads, Highways, or Bridges; Horses or Carriages employed in
carrying Manure (save Lime) for improving Lands, or Ploughs, or implements of
Husbandry; Horses employed in Husbandry, going to or returning from Plough,
or to or from Pasture, or Watering place, or going to be or returning from being
Shod; and Horses not going or returning on those occasions more than
two miles on the Turnpike Road, on which the exemption is claimed; Persons going
to or returning from, their proper parochial Church or Chapel; Persons going to
or returning from, their usual place of religious worship tolerated by Law, on
Sundays, or on any day on which Devine Service is ordered to be Celebrated;
Inhabitants of any Parish or Township going to, or returning from attending the
Funeral of any Person who shall die or be buried in the Parish, Township, or Hamlet, in
which any Turnpike Road shall lie, any Rector, Vicar, or Curate, on his parochial duty
within his Parish; Horses, Carts, or Waggons, conveying Vagrants sent by passes, or
any Prisoner sent by legal warrant; Horses or Carriages conveying the Mails;
Horses of any Officer or Soldier on march or duty; Horses or Carriages conveying
the Arms or Baggage of any such Soldiers or Officers, or returning therefrom or
any Sick, Wounded, or disabled Officers, or Soldiers, or any Ordnance, or other public
Stores; Horses and Carriages used by Corps of Yeomanry or Volunteers; Horses or
Carriages carrying or conveying any person to and from County Elections;
any Horse carrying any Agricultural produce which shall have grown on Land
in the occupation of or cultivated, used, or enjoyed by the Owner of such
produce, and which shall not have been sold; Sheep going to be washed;
Horses drawing or not drawing, which shall not pass more than three
hundred yards along the Turnpike Road.

A A toll-gate together with details of the tolls payable and the exemptions. The toll-gate can be seen at the Museum of Welsh Life

On the night of 6 June 1839, rioters attacked the toll-gates at Efailwen in Dyfed. Some had blackened their faces and others were dressed in women's clothes. What was it that made the country people of West Wales behave in such a way?

Many country roads were badly rutted and barely passable. As the number of horse-drawn coaches and waggons using the roads increased, something had to be done to improve matters. The answer was to set up Turnpike Trusts. Established by Acts of Parliament, the trusts were allowed to set up gates and charge tolls for the use of the roads. The Turnpike Trusts were run like small businesses and keepers were placed at the gates to collect the tolls.

Many of the toll-gates were on roads leading to markets or **lime-kilns,** which were busy places used regularly by farmers. Sometimes farmers even had to pay a toll to move animals from one farm to another! A toll paid at one gate only allowed the traveller to pass through the gates of that trust and another toll had to be paid at the next gates. There were different rates for different animals and for various types of carriages. There were also some exemptions.

Unpopular as they were, the toll-gates were not the only cause for complaint among country people. Wages were low and farm labourers struggled to feed their families. Those who had nothing lived in fear of being sent to the workhouse. People were angry because they had to pay a tax called a tithe to the Church. They also thought the Game Laws, which punished those caught poaching, were very unfair. With so many grievances, it is easy to see why the payment of tolls was the last straw.

The toll-gates at Efailwen were owned by the Whitland Trust and run by an Englishman named Thomas Bullin. The gatekeeper was Bullin's brother! The leader of the men who attacked the gates was a farmer, Thomas Rees, better known as *Twm Carnabwth* (Tom Stone Cottage). It is said that when he led the attack on the toll-gates, he wore clothes borrowed from a tall and stout woman named Rebecca. It is a good story, but it is more likely those who joined him took their name from a verse in the Bible. (See the box below).

There was peace for a while but in 1842 the troubles started again. The leaders of the rioters were John Jones (known as *Shoni Sgubor Fawr*) and David Davies (known as *Dai'r Cantwr*).

Shoni Sgubor Fawr was a tough, hard-drinking ex-soldier who came from Penderyn near Hirwaun. A well-known fist fighter, he

And they blessed Rebecca, and said unto her, Thou art our sister, be thou the mother of thousands of millions, and let their seed possess the gate of those which hate them.
(Genesis XXIV. v.60)

B *(left)* A contemporary artist's impression of the Rebecca rioters attacking a toll-gate

Probably the rest of your life will be spent in a foreign land ... You will be compelled to work but will receive no payment ... You will be, not in name but in reality, slaves. The sentence is that you, John Jones, will be transported beyond the seas for the rest of your natural life, and that you, David Davies, be tranported for twenty years.

C The sentences passed on Shoni Sgubor Fawr and Dai'r Cantwr

was a bully of a man who had once ruled Merthyr Tydfil's roughest area, China. When he moved to west Wales, his services were hired by those who wanted to see the end of the toll-gates. Dai'r Cantwr (David the Singer) was a different sort of man. He had worked in the mines and was a popular singer of ballads, as well as a part-time Methodist preacher. Sadly, he became a friend of Shoni. The two men not only attacked the toll-gates but also took to threatening and robbing others, including those who had hired them! When the authorities asked for help, soldiers were sent to the area to restore law and order. Although rewards were offered, the rioters were seldom caught.

Shoni and Dai were finally betrayed. At their trial, both pleaded guilty to a number of crimes. Chained together, the two men laughed as they were taken from the courtroom. The judge passed a tough sentence on them. (See source C).

The fate of Shoni remains a mystery but Dai'r Cantwr was pardoned, and he eventually returned to Wales. Back home, he lived as a tramp until his death in 1874. Drunk and sleeping rough in a barn, his pipe set the hay on fire and he died in the blaze.

The Rebecca riots were not altogether in vain. In 1843, the government agreed to look into the problems of the Turnpike Trusts and the toll-gates.

Oh sad is my fate; I am an object of pity to all who knew me; I have lost the good name I once possessed: heavy is my sorrow; ... instead of freedom, a long bondage is my lot: I must bid a long, a last farewell to my father's house where I received so much kindness in my infancy.

D The words of part of a farewell song written by Dai'r Cantwr

---

1 In what ways might farmers have tried to cheat the tolls?

2 Look at source B.
   (a) Do you think that the artist was on the side of the rioters or the turnpike owners?
   (b) How reliable do you feel the picture is?

3 'Just a load of troublemakers wanting a fight.' Does the evidence in this chapter support such a view?

4 Using this and earlier chapters, make a list of the main complaints working people may have had at this time?

13 Towpaths, locks and barges

In the new industrial age, it was important to find a cheap way of moving bulky goods like iron and coal from place to place. The roads could not cope and rivers were only navigable for parts of their length. The answer lay in building canals.

James Brindley and the Bridgewater Canal

The great canal builder James Brindley was a strange man. He could hardly read or write, and it is said that when he faced a problem he would go to bed for days on end, finally emerging with an answer. The Duke of Bridgewater asked Brindley to build a canal to connect his coalmines at Worsley, with Manchester. The Bridgewater Canal was opened in 1776. With his transport costs cut by half, the Duke was able to reduce the price of his coal but still increase his profits! The completion of the Bridgewater Canal started a period of frantic canal building as others tried to achieve the same advantages.

In order to build a canal it was first necessary to get the approval of Parliament. Once the money had been raised, men had to be found to do the digging. The labourers, known as navigators or 'navvies' for short, came from all over the country, and many were Irish. They worked with picks and shovels and each was expected to move 10 cubic metres of earth daily. The bottom and the sides of the canals had to be watertight and this was done by stamping down layer after layer of a **sludge** made of a mixture of clay and sand. To cope with the problem of gradient, locks had to be constructed to allow barges to pass from one level to another. Large numbers of **aqueducts** and tunnels also had to be built.

Canals appeared everywhere. By 1830, a network of man-made waterways had spread 3,000 kilometres across the country. The Grand Trunk Canal made it possible to cross the country from the North Sea to the Irish Sea, the Grand Junction Canal connected London with the Midlands and the Kennet and Avon Canal joined the River Thames with the River Severn.

The Glamorganshire Canal

The canal, started in 1790, took eight years to complete and cost £103,000. It ran from Merthyr Tydfil to Cardiff and there were fifty locks along its 40 kilometre course. Abercynon, known at different times as The Basin and Navigation, was a mass of wharves and warehouses. It was important as 'the clearing house of iron for the world.'

To the east, a canal joined Crumlin and Newport whilst the Brecknock and Abergavenny Canal served the Gwent valleys. In West Wales, the Swansea Canal went as far north as Ystalyfera. The most impressive canals in North Wales were the Montgomeryshire

A The flight of locks on the Glamorganshire Canal at Abercynon

We used to sit on the bridge and watch the barges pass pulled by horses ... The most exciting time was when there was a storm and the lock keeper had to put planks across the canal to avoid a flood. One section ... near Hawthorn was very prone to flooding.

B Mary Powell's memories of the canal, quoted in *Memories of the Glamorgan Canal* by Elis Owen

The shape of the machine resembles a Noah's Ark ... Two horses, harnessed one before the other, tow it along at the rate of a league an hour: a pace which is pleasant to keep up with when walking on the bank. The canal is just wide enough for two boats to pass. England is now intersected in every direction by canals.

C In 1807, the writer, Robert Southey described the working of a canal

and Ellesmere Canals.

On the broader canals, the old river barges were able to operate but elsewhere narrow boats were used. Horses using the tow-paths pulled them along at a speed of 3 or 4 kilometres an hour. They had to be 'walked' through tunnels by 'leggers' - men who lay on their backs and pushed against the roof with their feet. Like the turnpike roads, the canal companies charged tolls. Some companies operated their own boats and also made money from freight charges. Boats called 'hobblers' were privately owned and plied for hire.

The building of the canals gave work to over 50,000 men. The canals provided an important system of transport which was cheap and reliable. They were a good way of moving bulky and heavy goods to markets and ports.

Sadly canals also had disadvantages. Movement was very, very slow and the locks and tunnels caused delays. They were no good for conveying goods which were needed urgently or likely to perish. They were not suited for passenger travel and, although used for the purpose, not ideal for moving livestock. When the time came, canals were in no position to compete with the railways.

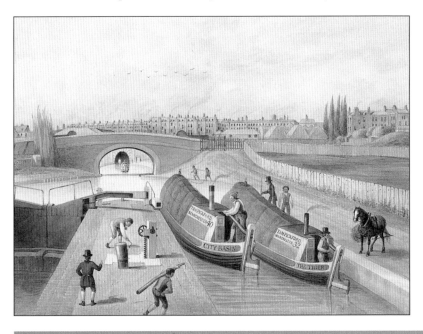

O! Could I make verses with humour and wit,
George Tennant, Esquire's great genius to fit;
From morn until even, I would sit down and tell,
And sing the praise of the Neath Junction Canal.

Now this will improve the trade of the place,
I hope that the business will daily increase;
All sorts of provisions we shall have to sell,
Convey'd us in boats by Neath Junction Canal.

D Two verses from a ballad written about the Neath Junction Canal, by Elizabeth Davies, who ran a lollipop shop in Swansea

E (left) A painting by T H Shepherd (c 1825) shows boats carrying general cargo on the Regent's Canal

1 (a) What advantages did canals have over turnpike roads?
  (b) Who might object to canals and why?

2 Using sources A, B and C, what problems are referred to with regard to canals, which were not features of turnpike roads?

3 Look at source E.
  (a) Do you feel that this gives a favourable view of the canals? Give reasons for your answer.
  (b) Does the fact that this was painted much later than the events it shows make it useless to the historian? Give reasons for your answers.

$I4$ Disease and poverty

The Industrial Revolution brought with it a number of serious social problems. As we saw in Chapter 7, houses were built cheaply and with poor sanitation there was always the risk of disease and epidemics. Those who were old, unemployed or for other reasons unable to support themselves, were likely to end up in the workhouse. Homes had no clean water and only the most basic sanitation. Instead of flush toilets, sewage ran from **privies** into open cesspits. These were emptied by men who, because of the awful stench, worked after dark. They were known as 'night-men'. their carts leaked and left an unpleasant trail as they went through the streets.

In some industrial areas, there was no sanitation at all and men and women used the nearby waste tips! Sewage was also allowed to flow into the rivers. These were the very same rivers from which people took drinking water and the water needed to wash themselves and their clothes!

There was no refuse collection and open areas were strewn with rubbish and waste. Even arrangements for the burial of the dead were not strictly controlled.

Disease and epidemics

It was not surprising that such conditions encouraged rats, fleas and lice. Homes were filthy and people were dirty, often infested with all sorts of **parasites** due to a lack of soap and changes of clothing. There were outbreaks of smallpox, typhoid and typhus, but cholera was the most feared of all. Cholera is a very infectious disease,

A This sketch of workers' cottages in Preston appeared in a report on housing in 1844. The cesspool running between the rows of houses was emptied only twice a year

There were a great many long alleys. They were narrow ... like a tobacco pipe. In these alleys lived from 200 to 300 people, and there was but one privy for the whole of that number, and that was at the end. It was so horrible that no-one could approach it.

B From a report written by Lord Shaftesbury during the 1840s, in which he described a street in London's East End

C *(right)* A *Punch* cartoon of 1858 shows the state of the River Thames

caused by drinking foul water. Of those who caught the disease, over half died. There were major outbreaks of cholera in 1832, 1848, 1853 and 1866.

Another killer was tuberculosis. Called 'consumption', since it wasted away or consumed its victims, it was the result of living in dank, unventilated houses. As we shall see, there were men concerned about the welfare of working people and their families who tried to do something about the situation.

D *(right)* This artist's impression of inner-city squalor was called 'A court for King Cholera' (1852)

E This chart gives details of conditions in the homes of some of the first victims of the 1866 epidemic in Merthyr Tydfil

No.	When taken ill.	When died.	Where died.	Sex.	Age.	Occupation.	Circumstances.	Habits.	Any evidence of contagion or infection.	State of the Dwellings or Neighbourhood.
1	22nd August...	24th August ...	15, David square, Abercannaid	M.	36	Wife of Puddler ... (Welsh)	Very poor	Dirty	No possible contact ...	Damp, dirty, and unventilated.
2	22nd ,, ...	25th ,, ...	57, Quarry row, Tydfil's Well	F.	45	Wife of Fireman ... (Irish)	Poor	Dirty	ditto ...	Dirty, unventilated—yard at back most filthy.
3	23rd ,, ...	25th ,, ...	31, do do ..	M.	32	Fireman................. (Welsh)	Good	Clean and regular	ditto ...	A drain, which carries away house slops from houses above, runs under the house.
4	23rd ,, ...	26th ,, ...	13, Morris court, Merthyr	F.	75	Rag cleaner .... (Irish)	Poor	Clean	As a rag cleaner might have picked infected clothes	An untrapped gully at end of court, also heaps of ashes steeped with excrement, &c. House, no ventilation.
5	24th ,, ...	25th ,, ...	7, Cwm Canol street, Dowlais	M.	21	Hooker in Iron Mills (Irish)	Young Irish Labourer	Regular	No possible contact ...	Cesspool at back of house above level of lower floor—offensive.
6	24th ,, ...	25th ,, ...	1, Flag & Castle ct., Dowlais	M.	8	Son of Labourer ... (English)	Very poor ...	Dirty	ditto ...	Court unpaved, no convenience, earth sodden with house refuse.
7	24th ,, ..	1st September	16, Sunny Bank, Tydfil's Well	F.	53	Wife of Tailor .... (Welsh)	Very poor ...	Intemperate & Dirty	ditto ...	Cesspool in garden overflowing, floor of sleeping room thickly covered with dirt and filth.
8	25th ,, ...	27th August ...	1, Miles' court, Caedraw	F.	50	Wife of Hawker ... (Scotch)	Poor	Clean and regular	Her husband and herself travelled about the neighbouring towns—had been in Aberdare	Cesspool near house overflowing.
9	26th ,, ...	30th ,, ...	8, Coffin's ct., George Town	F,	80	Wife of Skinner ... (Welsh)	Poor	Very clean ...	Had attended her son, case No. 3	Unventilated—common cesspool in gardens full.
10	27th ,, ...	1st September	4, Lewis' square, Abercannaid	F.	32	Wife of Collier .... (Welsh)	Comfortable .	Clean and regular	Apparently spontaneous	Overcrowded with family and lodgers—9 out of the 12 attacked, 7 died. At back of bedroom heap of ashes foul with excrement.
11	28th ,, ...	1st ,, ...	9, Sunny Bank	F.	42	Wife of Labourer ... (Irish)	Comfortable .	Clean	May have visited case No. 7	Uncealed cow shed under the house in a most filthy state.
12	3rd September	5th ,, ...	12, Mt. Pleasant, Penydarren	F,	21	Wife and of Daughter Collier (Welsh)	Comfortable .	Clean	No known contact ...	Unceiled cow shed under the house in a most filthy state.
13	6th ,, ...	8th ,, ...		F,	8					

1 Look at source A. This was published as part of an official report. What message does it appear to be giving?

2 Look at sources C and E.
   (a) Either draw or explain what you would put in a cartoon which would give a similar message to that in source C.
   (b) What does source E show about the link between cholera and poverty?
   (c) Does source E suggest that people in Merthyr Tydfil knew about the causes of cholera in 1866?

3 How is the artist in source D trying to convince people that something urgently needs doing?

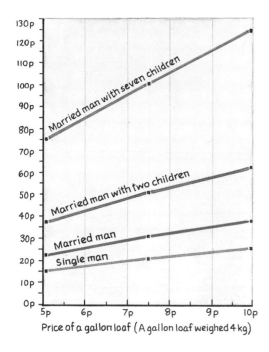

Price of a gallon loaf (A gallon loaf weighed 4 kg)

A The minimum wage was calculated according to the price of bread

B An artist's impression of the inside of a workhouse in the 1840s

Dealing with poverty

For one reason or another, there have always been poor people. For centuries, it had been the duty of each parish to look after its own poor. A tax, known as a Poor Rate, was paid by all landowners and this was used to help paupers. In some areas, workhouses were built to accommodate the poor. They included not only those unable to find work but also men and women who were too old, or too sick, to work, as well as unmarried mothers and orphans. The amount of money that had to be raised depended on the number of poor in the parish. It is easy to see why travelling beggars and tramps were not welcome and were likely to have dogs set on them. Some parishes did not bother to build workhouses. In 1792, a law was passed which allowed parishes to join together and share the cost of running a workhouse.

The Speenhamland system

Enclosures and the end of the war against France, added to the number of unemployed. In addition, there were a great many farm labourers living on low wages. As the price of bread rose, their position became desperate. To cope with the problem, a group of magistrates from the village of Speen in Berkshire put forward a plan by which workers received a minimum wage. This depended on the size of his family and moved up and down according to the price of a loaf of bread. Source A shows how the minimum wage was calculated.

The difference between a man's actual wage and the minimum wage to which he was entitled, was made up out of the Poor Rate. The idea caught on and was copied in other parts of the country. Unfortunately, the Speenhamland system, as it was called, was abused and became too expensive to run.

The government looked for a lasting solution to the problem of caring for the poor. In 1834, a law was passed, the Poor Law Amendment Act, which changed the system. Parishes now joined together to form 'Unions' and build workhouses. The workhouses were to be supervised by Poor Law guardians and paid for out of the rates. Although the old and sick still received help and were allowed to live in their own homes, able-bodied people were now only entitled to assistance if they went to the workhouses! The aim was to make life in the workhouse as harsh as possible so that people would prefer to find work, supporting themselves even if it meant living on low wages.

Workhouse life was extremely harsh. Men and women were separated and children taken from their parents. In addition to **paupers**, the workhouses took in beggars, tramps, orphans and the insane. The accommodation provided was cold and uncomfortable. Inmates slept on straw and were given food which was plain and limited in quantity. They had to eat in silence. They were not provided with underclothes and their outer garments were made of the roughest materials. There was only the most basic medical care. The day began at 6 a.m. and the work done was unpleasant and monotonous - usually breaking stones, picking oakum (untwisting rope) or crushing bones. Workhouse masters and matrons were hard taskmasters who bullied and abused the inmates. Little wonder the workhouses earned the nickname 'Poor Law **Bastilles**'.

From the start, there was opposition to the workhouses. William Cobbett thought the workhouses might cause a revolution, whilst Charles Dickens used his novel, Oliver Twist, to draw attention to the evils of the system.

The true horror of workhouse life was finally exposed when details of what was happening at a workhouse in Andover became known. There the master was Colin McDougal, an ex-sergeant major who had fought at the Battle of Waterloo. A drunkard, he treated his charges shamefully. Men and women at the workhouse were given work crushing bones so that they could be used to make glue. Some were so hungry that they scraped away the rotten meat they found left on the bones. It was even claimed that some bones came from the local graveyard!

Fortunately one of the workhouse guardians reported what he had heard to his Member of Parliament. An enquiry proved that all the terrible rumours told about the place were true. There was public outrage and, as a result, the old system came to an end. A Poor Law Board was set up and a member of the government appointed to keep an eye on things. Although workhouses remained inhospitable places, conditions gradually began to improve.

The workhouse should be a place of hardship, of coarse fare [food], a place of disgrace and humility; it should be run with strictness - with severity; it should be as repulsive as is consistent with humanity ...

C A clergyman expressed these views

D An engraving of the Andover workhouse during the nineteenth century

1 Look at sources A and C.
   (a) Using source A and other information in this chapter, how might people have been able to cheat the Speenhamland System?
   (b) Why is it surprising that the views in source C were expressed by clergyman?

2 Look at sources B and D and other information in the chapter.
   (a) Describe how bad conditions in the workhouse were.
   (b) How do you feel that people at the time should have tried to improve conditions in the workhouse?

3 Is it true to say that living conditions for all people living in Wales today are much better than they were at this time?

15 Victorian reformers

From what you have read, you might think that no one was concerned by the suffering of the men, women and children working in the factories and mines. This was not the case.

Ashley Cooper, Lord Shaftesbury

One of those who opposed the employment of young children in factories and mines was Anthony Ashley Cooper. Born into a rich family, an unhappy childhood made him aware of the suffering of others. Being a very religious man, he hated all forms of cruelty and neglect. Shaftesbury devoted his life to improving conditions in factories and mines. He also worked to provide education for working-class children, to prevent children being used as chimney sweeps and to help young criminals.

Laws had already been passed to limit the hours worked by children. With no inspectors to check what was happening, mill owners lied about the ages of their young workers or just simply ignored the law. In spite of fierce opposition, in 1833 Lord Ashley managed to get a law passed which said that no children under the age of nine were to be employed in mills. Furthermore, children under the age of thirteen were to work no more than forty-eight hours a week. Inspectors were also appointed to make sure the laws were obeyed. After 1836, all births and deaths had to be registered and this made it difficult for factory owners to cheat the system. Ashley next managed to get a **Royal Commission** set up to look into the condition of women and children who worked in coal mines. The report which followed shocked the nation. In 1842, Ashley's Mines Act made it illegal to employ women and young children underground. Five years later, the Ten Hours Act limited the hours worked by women and young people in the textile mills.

After Lord Shaftesbury's death in 1885, a memorial was erected to him in the centre of Piccadilly Circus - the statue of Eros.

Robert Owen's ideas

Robert Owen was a man who cared for his workers and showed how factories should be run. Born in 1771, at Newtown in Powys, he left home to work as a draper's assistant in London. A man of great drive and ambition, Owen moved to Manchester and went into business making spinning machines. He met and married the daughter of a wealthy Scottish mill owner and became manager of his father-in-law's mills at New Lanark. Owen believed that men were greatly affected by the environment in which they lived and worked. At the New Lanark mills, he refused to employ children under ten years of age or pauper apprentices, and cut the hours of his workers. Owen saw to it that his workers had reasonable homes

FACTORY ACT 1833

Banned children under 9 from working in textile mills

Banned anyone under 8 from night work

Appointed four factory inspectors

MINES ACT 1842

Banned women and children under 10 from working underground

Appointed inspectors

TEN HOURS ACT 1847

Maximum ten-hour day for women and those under 18

Maximum 58 hours a week

····AND ALSO

Help for the mentally ill and child chimney sweeps

A The reforms which Lord Shaftesbury helped to bring about

No Victorian was more ... guided by his conscience ... Men admired and put up with him when he behaved outrageously because they saw him holding ideals which few of them would have dared to carry to the same lengths.

B From a biography called *Shaftesbury*, by C F A Best (1964)

and was against the truck system. He set up a shop which sold 'articles of the best qualities supplied to people at the cost price'. He amazed other factory owners since, although he spent a great deal on improvements, his mills still made a good profit.

Robert Owen was not just a factory reformer, he was a man of ideals who wanted to create a fairer society, based more on co-operation than profit-making. He thought education was very important and set up a school for local children.

Owen also urged his workers and their families to join education classes and enjoy leisure activities. He put forward a plan to cure unemployment by building 'Villages of Co-operation', but was accused of wanting to put the unemployed in barracks. He even suggested that the price of goods should reflect how many hours it took to make them. He started to use 'labour notes' instead of money, with a value shown in 'labour hours'.

Unlike Lord Shaftesbury, Robert Owen was not a religious man but an atheist. He travelled widely and tried to set up **communes** in England and the United States, run on his socialist ideas. Owen also played a major part in the development of trade unions. In 1858, he died when visiting the town of his birth, Newtown. Owen is regarded as the 'Father of British Socialism'.

1 Learning should be natural and children should enjoy it

2 There was more to education than book learning

3 Children should not have to sit in tidy rows in classrooms but be allowed to roam freely

4 Children should not be punished or even suffer 'harsh, critical words'

C Robert Owen's ideas on education

D These cartoons show Owen's view that the behaviour of people was influenced by their environment

1 Why was Lord Shaftesbury likely to be unpopular with some people? Which people was he most likely to upset?

2 (a) What does the fact that Owen was able to surprise people suggest about beliefs at the time?
  (b) Look at source C. How many of Owen's ideas about education do you think are still sensible today?

(c) Divide Owen's ideas into those which you feel are sensible and those which are not. Compare your views with others in the class. Can you explain any differences in opinion?

3 Would you have been more convinced by Shaftesbury or Owen? Give reasons for your answer.

16 Slavery

For 300 years, Europeans took part in an unsavoury trade; shipping millions of native Africans across the Atlantic to sell them as slaves. British traders were among those who took part in this evil business.

The 'triangular trade'

Dealing in slaves was part of a 'triangular trade', with three connected voyages. On the first stage, ships took manufactured goods from Europe to the African coast where they were exchanged for slaves. On the second leg, or the 'middle passage', slaves were taken across the Atlantic to the West Indies where they were sold. Finally, the ships returned to Europe laden with cargoes of cotton, tobacco, sugar and rum. Once on the ships, the slaves were branded, chained and crammed together so that they filled every available space. The foul conditions led to outbreaks of diseases such as **scurvy** and smallpox.

Once in America, the slaves - men, women and children - were sold by auction. Buyers scrambled to inspect them, and were prepared to pay up to £60 for the strongest and the fittest. The more feeble were sold cheaply, whilst some, thought worthless because of their age or condition, were left on the waterfront to die.

Slaves had no rights and were the property of their masters. The cotton and sugar plantation owners thought it best to work them hard before they became useless. There was no profit in old slaves or those crippled by their hard labour. There were some who painted a happy picture of life on the plantations, claiming that slavery had brought the benefits of Christianity and civilisation to these people.

Trading in slaves produced great wealth. Fortunes were made as vast sums of money flowed into the country. To start with, Bristol was the centre of this prosperous trade in Britain, but the port was soon overtaken in importance by Liverpool. The merchants of that city were among the richest men in the country and they used their money to help finance the Industrial Revolution by investing their profits in canals and factories.

A This headstone on the grave of a slave can still be seen in a Bristol cemetery

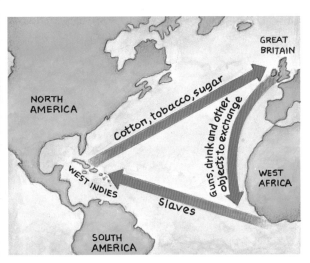

B The voyages which made up the 'triangular trade'

C *(right)* A picture taken from a book intended to make public the scandal of the over-crowding on British slaving ships

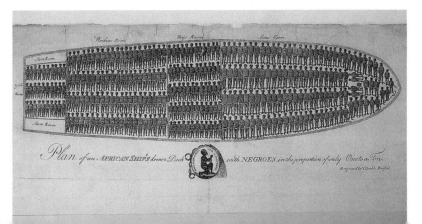

William Wilberforce and the abolition of slavery

William Wilberforce, a Member of Parliament and a deeply religious man, joined with others to set up a society opposed to slavery. A small man, but an impressive speaker, Wilberforce described slavery as a 'hateful traffic in human flesh' and devoted his life to campaigning for its abolition. Although he had a great deal of public support, he faced stiff opposition from plantation owners and traders, whose profits would suffer if their slaves were set free. Even so, in 1807, Parliament made it an offence for British subjects to take part in the slave trade, but it was not until 1833 that slavery was finally **abolished** throughout the British Empire. Wilberforce lived just long enough to hear that his cause had been won.

... we were all pent up together like so many sheep ... On the beat of a drum, the buyers rushed in to make a choice of those they like best ... In this manner are friends and relations separated ... never to see each other again.

E Olaudah Equiano, a slave who won his freedom, remembered being offered for sale. Quoted in *The British Empire*, BBC (1972)

D A poster advertising an auction of slaves

... unmerciful whippings continued until the poor creatures had not the power to groan in their misery ... I have seen them agonising under the torture of the thumbscrews.

F An account by John Newton, a former slave dealer who became a clergyman. Quoted in *The British Empire*, BBC (1972)

1 Using the information in this chapter, explain who you think made most money from the slave trade.

2 Look at source C.
(a) Do you think that this source was drawn by an opponent or a supporter of the slave trade?
(b) Work out what types of slaves were most likely to be wanted by the owners. Explain your answer.

3 What were the similarities and differences between the lives of working people in Britain at this time and slaves?

4 Which types of people might Wilberforce have had the greatest difficulty trying to convince that slavery was wrong?

17 From tramroads to railways

Great crowds assembled at Penydarren ... On the locomotive was Richard Trevithick ... A signal was given; a jet of steam burst forth, the wheels revolved ... the mass moved.

A In his *History of Merthyr Tydfil*, Charles Wilkins describes what happened on 12 February 1804

B A painting, by Terence Cuneo, shows the first journey of Trevithick's locomotive

I've navvied here in Scotland, I've navvied in the south,
Without a drink to cheer me or a crust to cross my mouth,
I fed when I was workin' and starved when out on tramp,
And the stone has been me pillow and the moon above me lamp,
I've done it like a navvy, a bold navvy man,
And I've done me graft and stuck it like a bold navvy man.

C Part of a song written by a navvy named 'Two-shift Mulholland'

In his book, Rural Rides, William Cobbett wrote that he had met a woman aged thirty-two who had never travelled more than four kilometres from her own home. This would not have been unusual - but then came the railways!

First came the tramroads, horse-drawn wagons pulled along wooden rails. One of the early tramroads in Wales connected the Swansea Canal with Oystermouth. It followed the route later taken by the Mumbles Railway. The first steam locomotive in Wales was built by a Cornishman, Richard Trevithick.

At eight kilometres per hour, the engine travelled from Penydarren to Abercynon. Afterwards, other famous locomotives were built, including Trevithick's Catch Me Who Can, William Hedley's Puffing Billy and George Stephenson's Rocket. The Liverpool to Manchester Railway was opened in 1830 and its success led to a rush to build railways.

The construction of the railway lines, with the building of bridges and embankments and the blasting of tunnels, was done by teams of remarkable men, the railway navvies. As tough as they come, dressed in moleskin trousers, coloured waistcoats and hob-nailed boots, they all had nicknames - 'Gypsy Joe', 'Thick-lipped Blondin' and 'Fighting Jack'.

In 1830, there were only 157 kilometres of track in the country. How the railway system grew! By 1880, a network of 25,000 kilometres of railtrack covered the country.

D Railway navvies of the 1840s

The railway companies offered first, second and third class travel. First class travel was elegant, but third class passengers stood in uncovered carriages and had to hold on to a handrail! In dark tunnels ladies put pins in their mouths to prevent amorous gentlemen kissing them! There was great rivalry between the railway companies. The carriages of each company were a different colour and their employees were all dressed in smart uniforms.

The railways in Wales

In 1841, the great engineer, Isambard Kingdom Brunel, was appointed to build the Taff Vale Railway, from Merthyr to Cardiff. Later, when working for the Great Western Railway, he was to be largely responsible for the line which connected London with South Wales passing through Newport, Cardiff and Swansea on its way to Milford Haven.

Davies, Stephenson and the Welsh railways

Before becoming involved in coalmining, David Davies had formed the Cambrian Railway to bring trains to mid-Wales. Later, he built a line to connect the Valleys with the new docks he was building at Barry. In North Wales, George Stephenson built the Britannia Bridge over the Menai Straits.

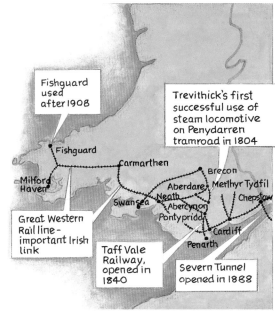

E The railways of South Wales to 1856

F (below) This illustration shows the changes brought about by the coming of the railways

1 Describe the possible feelings of someone at Penydarren who was seeing a steam train for the first time in their lives.

2 Look at sources C and D.
(a) What can you learn from source C about the views of navvies?
(b) Does source D give a favourable view of the navvies? Give reasons for your answer.

3 Why did some people oppose the railways in their area even though they were so useful for moving people and goods?

4 The railways brought a number of changes to Wales.
(a) List those which would have been noticed immediately.
(b) List those which brought change over a longer period.

Education for a few

At the start of the nineteenth century, there was no national system of education. The general view held was that it was not necessary to educate working-class children.

Knowledge could be a dangerous thing. If working-class children remained ignorant, they would grow to accept their position in life and show respect to those said to be their superiors. Educate them and they might try to 'rise above their station'. A report of 1816 warned that to educate the lower orders 'might do them a great deal of harm, it would enable them to read ... and that would tend to inflame their passions'! Queen Victoria said that education, 'rendered the working classes unfitted for good servants and labourers.'

A *(below)* **A Dame school. Although the old lady has fallen asleep, she still clutches a birch in her hand!**

Some teachers ... taught nothing but reading and spelling ... geography and history were scarcely ever seen in a school. Large numbers never entered the door of a schoolhouse ... Writing was looked upon as a luxury for the rich only. A person who was a good reader was looked up to by the people and said to be a 'great scholar'.

B Recollections of school days in the 1820's. From *Progress in Pudsey*, by Joseph Lawson

Many types of schools

Some young children could go to Dame schools. They were usually run by old women in their own homes and were little more than a child-minding service.

In some areas, local factory owners set up schools. Lord Shaftesbury raised money to support Ragged schools for very poor children. In addition to learning, these schools also provided food and clothing. For many children, the only education they would ever receive would be from a Sunday school. There were also charity schools run by religious groups, National schools for church children and British schools for those who went to chapel. In 1850, half the population of Wales and England could still not read or write. For those able to go to school, the range of subjects taught and the quality of teaching varied greatly.

Most schools offered a basic education in the 'The Three Rs' - Reading, wRiting and aRithmetic. The monitorial system was used to teach pupils. First, the teacher instructed the older, more intelligent children. Then they, as monitors, taught groups of younger children. Learning was 'by rote' - by repeating until subjects were remembered. Until they were able to use pen and ink, children were given slates and chalk to write with.

Children from better-off families had a wider choice of schools. A sound education in Greek and Latin was provided by grammar schools founded long before, with money given by kings, noblemen and merchants. The sons of the wealthy were sent to public schools. These had a reputation for bullying and rowdy behaviour. Thanks to men like Thomas Arnold, who was headmaster of Rugby, discipline improved as the schools turned more to learning and character training. Besides grammar and public schools, there were a range of badly run private boarding schools. In Nicholas Nickleby, Charles Dickens described life at Dotheboys Hall run by the awful Wackford Squeers.

The view that children should be strictly disciplined is shown in some popular sayings of the time - 'Spare the rod and spoil the child', and, 'Children should be seen and not heard.'

Right up the school through all six standards ... you did nothing but reading, writing and arithmetic. What a noise there used to be! Children reading aloud, teachers scolding, infants reciting, all louder and louder until the master rang the bell on his desk.

C Joseph Ashby's memories of going to the National School in his village. From *Learning and Teaching in Victorian Times*, by P F Speed (1964)

D *(below)* The monitorial system in use in a classroom

1 **Using the sources and other information in this chapter, what might a typical day consist of for a child or a teacher? Include in your account, what might happen and your feelings about the conditions.**

2 **Are there any ways in which schools have not changed between the nineteenth century and today?**

The mode of teaching writing is to set the few children in a school, who can afford copy-books, to copy, as best they can, either engraved script or written copies; usually the latter. The inattention of the master is generally manifested by the misspelling which grows down the page, and often by the increasing badness of the writing. I think I have seen three instances of Mulhauser's copy-books in use, and three only.

A An extract from the Blue Books, commenting on children's handwriting

... the Welsh language should be taught exclusively during one hour every School day and shall during the time be the sole medium of communication in the School.

B A statement by the founders of Llandovery College in 1848

C A cartoon makes fun of the three commissioners and Kay-Shuttleworth, the Secretary for Education who sent them to Wales

Education in Wales
'The Treason of the Blue Books'

In 1846, William Williams, the Welsh-born MP for Coventry, called for a commission to be set up to look into standards of education in Wales. Three young lawyers were sent from London to carry out the investigation. Afterwards, they wrote a report which was very critical of Welsh schools especially their teachers, the way they taught and the school buildings. Even worse, the report described Welsh as 'the language of slavery', claiming that the use of the Welsh language was 'a vast drawback to Wales' and a 'barrier to the ... progress and prosperity of the Welsh people.' The report even went as far as to criticise the behaviour of Welsh women and said that the people of Wales were given to drinking and dishonesty!

There was a lot wrong with education in Wales, but the criticism of the Welsh people and their language was thought to be biased and very unfair. The report led to a great deal of anger and hostility. The commissioners who prepared the report did not themselves speak Welsh. A report written by Parliament was called a 'Blue Book' because of the colour of its cover. Afterwards, people spoke of 'The Treason of the Blue Books' (*Brad y Llyfrau Gleision*) and the books were regarded as an insult to the Welsh people.

The report did, however, cause people to look more closely at the state of education in Wales. The number of schools grew steadily and new **endowed** schools appeared.

After the scandal of the Blue Books, it became a custom that any child caught speaking Welsh was likely to be punished by having a piece of wood or slate hung around his or her neck with the letters WN - Welsh Not - cut into it. The child wore it until it could be passed on to the next one caught speaking Welsh. Even so, there were still those willing to stand up for their language.

Payment by results

Meanwhile other changes were taking place nationally. In 1858, another commission suggested that teachers should be paid

according to how well they taught their pupils. Inspectors went to each school to question children in their classes. With their pay at stake, teachers made the children memorise their tables and masses of facts, even more thoroughly. Teachers also found ways of beating the system such as encouraging backward pupils to stay away when the inspectors were due! The man whose idea it was said of the system 'If it is not cheap, it shall be efficient and, if it is not efficient, it shall be cheap.'

Further improvements

A big step forward came in 1870 when School Boards were set up. The Boards supervised schools in their own area and were expected to build schools in areas where there were none. The schools, which received money from the government and from the rates, were to be regularly inspected. The law also said that all chidren between the ages of five and twelve had to attend school. Now elementary education was compulsory, attendance officers had to be appointed to round up truants. They were nicknamed 'Boardmen', 'kiddie catchers' or 'whippers-in'.

D The teacher and children at Grangetown Board School, Cardiff in 1897

 E A reconstruction of a Victorian classroom at the Museum of Welsh Life, St Fagans

1 Using source A and other information in this chapter, how can you support the view that many of the educational changes were not helpful to people in Wales?

2 Look at source E. Can we be sure that all Victorian classrooms in Wales looked like this reconstruction?

3 'Education at this time was all useless.' Say whether you agree with this opinion.

19

*T*o church or to chapel?

The mid-eighteenth century saw the development of a new interest in religion in Wales. It was the time of a great awakening when people took to reading the Bible and going to chapel regularly.

Anglicans and Noncomformists

In Wales, the official or 'established' church was the Church of England. People who belonged to the Church were called **Anglicans**. People who did not agree with the beliefs of the Church, or like the way Anglicans conducted their services, were called Dissenters. Later they were known as Nonconformists - people who did not go along with, or conform to, the Church's ways.

The Methodists

Anglican clergymen were very poorly paid. Some took little interest in the people and neglected their parishes. Even so, among them there were also good, caring men who were strict in their beliefs. They travelled about and preached at open air meetings. Because of their strict and ordered approach to religion, they were called Methodists. They preached with great spirit and attracted large crowds. In England, the leaders of the Methodist movement were the hymn writing brothers, John and Charles Wesley. In Wales, the leading Methodists were Howell Harris, Daniel Rowland and another famous hymn writer, William Williams who lived on a farm, Pantycelyn, near Llandovery.

Williams's hymns remain popular today. The words of *Cwm Rhondda*, sung by crowds at Welsh rugby internationals, are taken from Williams's hymn, *Guide me O Thou Great Jehovah*. For as long as it was possible, the Methodists stayed within the Church of England but the differences between them became too great and in 1811, they broke away to form a separate group of Nonconformists. They built their own chapels and appointed their own ministers.

Church or chapel?

Broadly speaking, most of the English-speaking landowners remained loyal to the Church of England whilst the bulk of ordinary, Welsh-speaking people became Nonconformists. In towns and villages, people thought more seriously about religious matters and went to chapel to hear the great preachers, like John Elias, John Jones, Tal-y-sarn, and the Baptist, Christmas Evans. A census taken in 1851 showed that 80 per cent of Welsh people who attended a place of worship were Nonconformists. There is no better example than that of Mary Jones to show how seriously people took religion.

A The grave of William Williams, Pantycelyn at Llanfair Church, Llandovery

That was a hard road I found to make a living in the service of God ... And yet, brother, a man may enter a bank in a fine suit but it is the tattered paper in his hand ... that gives him access to the treasure of the vault. If you can only believe - everything comes to him who believes.

B An extract from a sermon by Christmas Evans

Mary Jones of Llanfihangel-y-pennant

Mary Jones was a weaver's daughter from Llanfihangel-y-Pennant in Gwynedd. Although unable to go to school, she had learned to read by the age of ten. Her family were too poor to own a Welsh Bible, so she borrowed one from a neighbour. Over a period of six years, she saved the seventeen pence necessary to buy one of her own. Aged sixteen, she walked barefooted across the forty kilometres of the mountains to Bala to buy a Bible from the Methodist minister, Thomas Charles. Sadly, he had no Bibles to spare but gave her one he had put aside for a friend. The Bible was her constant companion until she died in 1872 at the age of 88. It is said that the girl's walk to Bala inspired Thomas Charles to support the setting up of the British and Foreign Bible Society.

A God-fearing people

It was largely because of the work of the Methodists that so many Welsh men and women became chapel goers. On Sunday, the chapels were full, with every pew taken. People of all ages attended Sunday school and, during the week, people gathered for prayer meetings. The Welsh had a new image - that of a strict, sober, God-fearing people.

Religion and politics

Ordinary people saw the Methodists as their champions against the wealthy landowners who were Anglicans and voted Tory (then the name for Conservatives). Welsh-speaking, chapel people gave their support to the other rival political party, the Liberals. In 1868, 21 Welsh Liberal MPs were elected to Parliament. The landlords took their revenge by throwing hundreds of farmers off their land. In 1872, a law made voting secret. This meant that the landowners could no longer tell how their tenants voted!

C *(right)* A comparison of the interiors of the St Nicholas parish church in the Vale of Glamorgan and that of the Pen-rhiw chapel at the Museum of Welsh Life

1 Look at source C. What are the main differences in the appearance of churches and chapels?

2 How can you explain why the Methodists had so much appeal in Wales?

3 (a) In what ways do you think the story of Mary Jones was so admired at the time?

(b) Do you think that it still arouses such feeling?

4 Using evidence from this and other chapters answer these questions:
a) How important was religion to people?
b) Did religion play a greater part than education in strengthening Welsh identity? (See Chapter 18).

20 *T*he reform of Parliament

Today, all men and women over the age of eighteen can vote to choose their Member of Parliament. This has not always been the case. At the start of the nineteenth century, ordinary people were not involved in politics since few men and no women had the right to vote.

The system before 1832

The old system of returning Members to Parliament had remained unchanged for hundreds of years. There were 'rotten' and 'pocket' boroughs. A 'rotten borough' was one which sent a Member to Parliament although the town no longer existed. Old Sarum, near Salisbury, was nothing more than a mound of earth and Dunwich on the Suffolk coast, had disappeared under the North Sea, yet both were represented in London by two Members of Parliament! A 'pocket borough' was one controlled by, or 'in the pocket of', a local lord, or landowner of influence. At Beaumaris, the Bulkeley family had provided the MP for over 150 years. The Morgan family represented Brecon for 80 years without a break!

The right to vote usually depended on whether people owned land or paid rates. At Brecon, only 17 men had the right to vote! There were odd exceptions. In a 'potwalloper borough', you could vote if you owned a home with a fireplace on which you could boil a pot! In 1830, no women at all and only one man in twelve had the right to vote! Even so, some thought there was no need for any major change.

A Old Sarum today

I am opposed to universal suffrage because I think it would produce a … revolution. We say … that it is not by mere numbers, but by property and intelligence that the nation ought to be governed.

B An argument put forward in 1831, by the historian Thomas Macaulay

C *(right)* George Cruikshank's cartoon shows what happened on polling day. You can see the ways in which the candidate, 'Pilfer', is trying to persuade people to vote for him

Constituencies, areas which elected MPs, varied in size. Towns, like Merthyr Tydfil, which had grown up during the Industrial Revolution, still had no Members to represent them. Constituencies were also of vastly different sizes. On polling day, there was no secrecy. The few people who had the right to vote did so openly. This meant that influential men who were keen to become Members of Parliament could bribe or threaten voters. The system was very **corrupt**.

No working-class men and few middle-class men had a say in the nation's affairs. The country was run by, and in the best interests of, the landed gentry. MP's were not paid, so only wealthy men could enter Parliament. Outspoken men demanded change. They wanted the vote to be given to many more people, MPs to be fairly shared out and for voting to be held in secret.

The storm over the Reform Act

In 1831, the Whig Party (or Liberals, as they were soon to be known) proposed changes which would improve matters. In Parliament, the Tories twice turned down their ideas. There were demonstrations, riots and great excitement across the country as MPs gathered to consider the matter for a third time. In some areas, soldiers had to restore law and order. It was only after the king became involved that the law was finally passed in June 1832.

The Great Reform Act, as the law was called, did bring some changes. Country areas lost their MPs and they were given to the new industrial towns. Wales gained five more seats in Parliament and for the first time Merthyr Tydfil and Swansea elected their own MPs. Although the vote was given to 50 per cent more men, it still only represented one man in every seven. In Merthyr, only 500 men could vote! Voting was not to be in secret so the threats and bribes continued as before. The people, who had expected so much, felt let down and were bitterly disappointed. Out of their anger was born a new movement - Chartism.

The town of Old Sarum, which contains not three houses, sends two members; and the town of Manchester, which contains upwards of sixty thousand souls, is not admitted to send any.

D From *Rights of Man*, by Thomas Paine

... his expenses amounted to £15,690 - 11,070 breakfasts, 36,901 dinners, 684 suppers, 25,275 gallons of ale, 11,068 bottles of spirits ... £686 for ribbons and 4,521 charges for horse hire.

E In his *A History of Modern Wales*, (1950), David Williams described how much it cost Sir William Paxton to try to get elected for Carmarthenshire. He still failed to win

---

1 (a) List the main types of people who could not vote before 1832.
 (b) Why do you think that wealthy people were so keen to be MPs?
 (c) What arguments do you think the wealthy might use to keep things as they were? (Source B may provide some useful clues).
 (d) Using information in this chapter, state how wealthy people tried to ensure that they were elected. (Source E may be helpful here).

2 Write a letter arguing a case for changing the voting system in 1831. You should include what ought to happen and why.

3 If the situation was so unfair, why do you think that nobody did much to improve things until the 1830s?

4 From the evidence provided in this chapter answer the following questions:
 (a) How satisfied do you think different types of people were after the Great Reform Act?
 (b) How might they react after 1832? Give reasons for your answer.

A A picture of William Lovett

B The Chartist demands

'Spread the Charter far and wide'

In 1840, John Frost - a successful Newport business man, Justice of the Peace and former mayor of the town - was brought to trial at Monmouth. Together with two others, he was sentenced to be hanged. Why was Frost, a good man who had served the local community well, being sent to the **gallows**? Frost was not only a radical and a Nonconformist, he was also one of the leaders of the Chartist movement in Wales.

As we have seen, there were a great many reasons why people were dissatisfied; low wages, poor working conditions, dreadful housing, the truck system, unemployment, the workhouses. If only it was possible to elect Members of Parliament who were willing to bring about change, things might be different. In 1832, people had high hopes that there would soon be greater fairness in the way Parliament was elected. The Reform Act of 1832 let them down badly. Disappointment turned to anger as working-class leaders thought of new ways to continue the struggle.

The People's Charter

In 1838, William Lovett drew up a People's Charter. In it, he listed six demands (see source B). Those who supported the six demands were called Chartists. Lovett was a quiet, gentle type of man who wanted to achieve the aims of the Charter by peaceful means. Others, led by Feargus O'Connor, were less patient and, if necessary,

SECRET VOTING BY BALLOT

No need for Members of Parliament to own property

MEMBERS OF PARLIAMENT TO BE PAID

VOTES FOR ALL MEN OVER 21

Each Member of Parliament to represent the same number of people

Parliamentary elections every year

were quite prepared to use violence. O'Connor was a red-haired, loud-voiced Irishman who spoke well and could easily hold the attention of a large crowd. He thought the government would only listen to the Chartists if they were frightened. In the north of England and the Midlands, working people attended Chartist meetings in large numbers. There were even rumours that men were being trained to use weapons.

The Welsh Chartists

In Wales, Chartism first appeared at Carmarthen and then at Llanidloes and Newtown, where local weavers were having a hard time. When it became known that some local men were gathering arms and practising drill, London policemen were sent to the area and, shortly afterwards, soldiers arrived from Brecon. A few men were arrested and three sentenced to be transported. Chartism was also well supported in South Wales where the Merthyr Riots and the hanging of Dic Penderyn were still fresh in people's minds. On top of this, there was a great deal of bad feeling between masters and men over the issue of trade unions. In Gwent, some workers who had been denied the right to form unions, organised themselves into lawless bands. Known as 'Scotch Cattle', they terrorised local people who sided with the masters by harassing them and burning down their homes. By far the most serious outbreak of violence occurred in Newport.

In 1839, the Chartists sent a petition to Parliament, listing all their aims. It was signed by over one and a quarter million people. The government turned it down immediately. The Chartists did not take defeat lightly and began to step up their activities.

We have resolved to obtain our rights, peaceably if we may, forcibly if we must; but woe to those who begin warfare with millions …

C A warning by Feargus O'Connor at a meeting in 1839

D A picture of Feargus O'Connor

The whole physical force agitation is harmful and injurious to the movement. Muskets are not what are wanted, but education and schooling of working people … O'Connor wants to take everything by storm.

E Lovett's reply to O'Connor's speech (see source C)

1 (a) How far do you feel the six demands of Lovett are reasonable?
(b) If the demands are generally very reasonable, why do you think that people opposed them at the time?

2 Why did people think that if the Charter succeeded it would lead to an improvement in their lives? Use the text and the sources to help you.

Newport, 1839: Riot or rising?

In a meeting held at the Coach and Horses Inn in Blackwood, local Chartists led by John Frost, Zephaniah Williams and William Jones, secretly made plans to hold a large demonstration in Newport on 3 November 1839. It was intended that three separate columns of men would march from Blackwood, Ebbw Vale and Pontypool and join together to march into Newport. Things went badly from the start. The weather was so awful that instead of the expected 20,000 marchers, only 5,000 turned up! They were soon drenched and many lost their enthusiasm and turned back. As the rain cleared, the men assembled at Tredegar Park for the final march into the centre of Newport. It was 8.30 am when the men made their way down Stow Hill and assembled before the Westgate Hotel. The mayor of Newport, Thomas Phillips, was ready for them. He read the Riot Act and stood with special constables in front of the hotel. Unknown to the demonstrators, he had also made arrangements for 30 armed soldiers to be hidden in the hotel. Suddenly there was a scuffle and a shot rang out. As the Chartists tried to force their way into the building, the shutters of the windows were thrown open and the soldiers fired three volleys into crowds outside. The mob stopped in its tracks, hesitated, then broke and ran. Nine were left dead outside the hotel.

The riot was as good as over. Throughout this time, the mayor had stood in the thick of it and was badly wounded in the arm. Thomas Phillips, himself a man of humble origins whose father had once worked on the cinder tips at Ebbw Vale, was later honoured by Queen Victoria for his bravery.

John Frost spent the rest of the day hiding in a coal truck at Castleton before making his way to the home of a friend, John Partridge. Within a few days all the ringleaders had been rounded up. They were brought to trial at Monmouth where they were charged with high treason.

The judge showed some sympathy for the Chartists and advised the jury to acquit them. The prosecution argued that the rising in Newport was not a demonstration but part of a much bigger

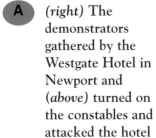

A *(right)* The demonstrators gathered by the Westgate Hotel in Newport and *(above)* turned on the constables and attacked the hotel

nationwide revolution. The jury agreed and found the men guilty. They were sentenced to death. After a number of appeals had been made on their behalf, their sentences were reduced to transportation for life. They were sent to the hulks (prison ships) in Portsmouth, on the first stage of their journey to Tasmania.

John Frost spent 15 years as a convict. Unfortunately part of a letter he wrote to his wife was published in a newspaper and because it criticised a member of the government, his sentence was increased by a further two years, this time with hard labour added! In 1854, Frost was pardoned on condition that he did not return to Britain. When he was finally allowed home, the people of Newport gathered to give him a great welcome. He went to live in Bristol and travelled the country giving talks about his experiences. He died in 1877 at the age of 93.

Other Chartist petitions

In 1842, a second petition with 3 million signatures was presented to Parliament. Like the first, it was thrown out. There were a few scattered strikes and riots but nothing more. Then, five years later, the movement suddenly came to life again. A new petition was organised, this time with 5 million signatures. The Chartist leaders planned to hold a mass meeting on Kennington Common and then march on Parliament with the petition. The government enlisted 150,000 special constables and brought troops and guns into London. They were used to guard the bridges in order to stop the Chartists crossing the River Thames. The petition was taken to Parliament in three cabs. When it was closely examined, it was found to contain less than 2 million signatures and many of these were obvious forgeries - Queen Victoria's signature appeared sixteen times together with that of the Duke of Wellington and Mr Punch! Once again the petition was turned down. Although Chartism became less important, it would be wrong to consider the movement a total failure. After 1858, MPs no longer had to own property; the majority of working men got the vote in 1870; secret voting was introduced in 1872 and, after 1911, MPs were paid.

TO THE
Working Men
OF
Monmouthshire.

COUNTRYMEN,

The scene which Newport yesterday presented to our view must, to every honest man, have been painful in the extreme. Numbers of men, of the working classes, with broken heads, and these wounds inflicted by Special Constables, sworn to preserve the Peace. Many of them Drunk, and under the command of a Drunken Magistrate. Numbers of Tradesmen of Newport, either aiding in assaulting Men, Women and Children, or silently witnessing, without any attempt to prevent those attacks on their unoffending neighbours. Is this the way in which the Mayor and the Magistrates of Newport preserve the peace? Was it to sanction actions of this description that the Soldiers were sent for to Newport? Will conduct of this sort produce no desire for revenge in those who suffer by it? Men of Monmouthshire, be cool, be patient; if justice be set aside: if Club Law is to be the order of the day, those who play at that game may find it a losing one.

My advice to you, working men of Monmouthshire is, be cool, but firm. We seek for nothing but our rights as members of a civil community. We have sought them peaceably; we still seek them peaceably. It is the object of our enemies to drive us to some outbreak in order to destroy us. This is the state in which our country is now placed. The people ask for bread, and the answer is the bludgeon or the sword. Let not the desire of the enemy be gratified.

Faithfully, your obedient Servant,

JOHN FROST.

John Partridge, Printer, Newport.

B A pamphlet prepared by John Frost, in which he gives his views of the events in Newport the day before

C A bust of John Frost

1 **Write a newspaper report on the Newport Riots, either supporting the Chartists or the Government. Sources A and B may be helpful in supporting one side or another. Do not just tell the story but remember to express some views supporting the side you have chosen.**

2 **Look at sources A and B Which of these sources do you think a historian trying to understand Chartism would find most useful? Give reasons for your answer.**

3 **Compare what happened to Frost with the case of Dic Penderyn (Chapter 11). Can you suggest any reasons why one was executed and the other was not?**

4 **Did Chartism fail? Think carefully, this is not as straightforward as it seems.**

21

A Crystal Palace or a 'Monstrous Greenhouse'?

Queen Victoria and her husband, Prince Albert

I would not flatter anybody, but ... having worked on the same board with His Royal Highness, I can speak of his efforts not as a prince but as a working man. He had before him ... as great an amount of labour ... as any workman in the Kingdom.

A A statement by Richard Cobden, a famous politician of the time

... unbelievably modern, incredibly beautiful ... So graceful, so delicate, so airy, it ... must defy all rivalry.

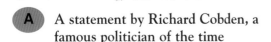

B Lord Redesdale's description of the Crystal Palace

In 1851, London was the scene of a spectacular trade show. The show was to display the latest industrial, scientific and artistic achievements of all the countries of the world. It was officially called The Great Exhibition of the Works of Industry of All Nations, but became better known as simply The Great Exhibition.

One of the people behind the idea to hold a Great Exhibition was the President of the Royal Society of Arts, Prince Albert, the husband of Queen Victoria. The Prince did not just lend his name to the venture but also worked hard to make sure it was a success. (See source A).

The exhibition, which was backed with money from industry and private individuals, was to be held in Hyde Park in London. Of the 250 plans submitted by various architects, the organisers chose the one put forward by Joseph Paxton.

Joseph Paxton's plans

Joseph Paxton, son of a Derbyshire farmer, came from a humble background. It was whilst working as a gardener that his skills attracted the attention of the Duke of Devonshire. The duke appointed him to design the gardens at Chatsworth and Paxton's idea for the main exhibition building, the Crystal Palace, came from the glass conservatory there. The building he aimed to construct was to cover nearly nine hectares. It was to be 500 metres long and reach a height of 33 metres. Some 300,000 panes of glass were going to be needed and great avenues were to run along each side of it.

Yet Paxton's plan had its critics. There were those who said that Hyde Park was the wrong place for such a large exhibition, since it might become 'the bivouac of all the vagabonds in London' and attract 'foreigners with all sorts of diseases'. As for the design, some unkindly referred to it as 'Mr Paxton's Monstrous Greenhouse'.

It took 2000 men, seventeen weeks to build the Crystal Palace. Among great splendour and pomp, the exhibition was opened by Queen Victoria on 2 May 1851.

The exhibition

From all over the world, 14,000 exhibitors put on show over 100,000 exhibits. Of course, British machinery and manufactured goods were an important part but half the area was given to the display of foreign goods; toys from Germany, textiles from France, furs from Russia, cotton goods from the United States, and woollen goods from Australia. Over 6 million people travelled to see the exhibition from all over the world. In Britain, some factory owners gave their workers time off and even paid for them to take their families to London. Of course, there were millions who could not go. The cost for a family would be more than a week's rent and they simply could not afford it.

The Great Exhibition stayed open for five and a half months before it finally closed on 11 October 1851. It made a clear profit of £186,437, a very large sum of money in those days. The money was put to good use. In Kensington, land was purchased on which to build the Science Museum, the Victoria and Albert Museum, the Royal Colleges of Art and Music and the Albert Hall.

The Crystal Palace was taken down and re-built at Sydenham in South London. Although destroyed by a fire in 1936, it remains famous as the home of a football club.

D An illustration of the Crystal Palace (1851)

C A famous cartoon of 1851, in which Mr Punch reminds Prince Albert that there were people unable to visit the Great Exhibition

... it was the greatest day in our history, the most beautiful and imposing and touching spectacle ever seen ... It was the happiest day of my life.

E An extract from one of Queen Victoria's letters

The exhibitors, by showing their dependence on each other, will be a happy means of promoting unity among nations, and peace and goodwill among the races of mankind.

F Prince Albert's view of the exhibition - a chance to show off the achievements of different countries

1 (a) In what ways were opinions divided about the Crystal Palace?
  (b) From the information in this chapter, can you see any likely problems with the building?

2 How useful are sources E and F in giving the views of people at the time?

3 Look at source C.
  (a) What impression is the artist trying to give?
  (b) Can you find evidence elsewhere in this chapter which either agrees or disagrees with this view?

4 'Just done to show off supposed British superiority.' Do you feel that this view of the Great Exhibition is true?

22

Years of the Empire

By the end of the nineteenth century, Britain ruled a vast empire which covered one third of the world. Maps had large areas coloured red (the British Empire) and people spoke of 'an empire on which the sun never set'.

The importance of having an overseas empire lay in the wealth it created. Colonies provided cheap **raw materials** and food, and also offered ready markets for manufactured goods. Empires were created by the discovery and exploration of new lands, and by war and conquest.

By the eighteenth century, the British Empire included much of North America, India, Australia and numerous islands scattered across the oceans. In 1776, the loss of the thirteen American colonies came as a bitter blow. In 1857, there was a mutiny against British rule in India, a colony looked upon as 'the jewel in the crown'. The mutiny was put down. The years after 1870 saw a rush to colonise Africa. Britain played a leading part in the 'Scramble for Africa' and, by 1900, owned colonies which stretched about the whole length of the continent.

During Queen Victoria's reign, thousands of people emigrated to Canada, Australia, New Zealand and South Africa. They included many Welsh families who were attracted by the prospect of plenty of open space and the chance of a freer and better way of life than they had at home. Not all went willingly. Some involved in the Merthyr riots and in the Rebecca and Chartist movements went by way of convict ships!

Native peoples resisted the take over of their lands by foreigners. The Aboriginal people of Australia, the Maoris of New Zealand were badly treated. In Africa, British armies had to fight campaigns against Ashanti, Matabele and Zulu peoples. In 1879, the 24th Foot, later the South Wales Borderers, were involved in a famous battle against the Zulus at Rorke's Drift. Regimental colours list the 'battle honours' of a regiment - the battles in which the regiment fought (see source B for those of the Royal Welch Fusiliers).

To defend the Empire and protect the sea routes between Britain and her overseas possessions, it was necessary to build a large and powerful navy. In those days, the ships of the Royal Navy really did 'rule the waves'. After the age of the fast **clipper** ships with their enormous sails, world trade was carried by steam ships. This meant that it was necessary to maintain coal depots along the important sea lanes. Welsh steam coal was much sought after by shipping companies and the Royal Navy because it was smokeless and prevented warships from giving away their position to the enemy.

In 1869, a French engineer, Ferdinand de Lesseps, finished building the Suez Canal. The canal linked the Mediterranean Sea

A This map shows the extent of the British Empire in 1900

B The colours of the Royal Welch Fusiliers

with the Red Sea and cut the travelling time between Europe and Asia by many days. Six years later, Disraeli, the British Prime Minister, managed to buy enough shares in the canal for Britain to control it. (See source C). The Suez Canal became an important link between Britain and her empire in the East.

Empire - the case for and against

Britain used her position at the centre of a large empire to great advantage. By the end of the nineteenth century, she was one of the richest and most powerful nations in the world.

Britain was not the only colonial power. France, Holland and Portugal also had empires. Some argued that the peoples of the colonies also benefited since they were brought into contact with learning and Christianity. The truth is that all people wish to be in charge of their own affairs. Colonial peoples saw themselves as being wrongly used, having the culture and religion of others forced upon them. They were not able to share in the wealth of their lands which was controlled by a colonising power. The British Empire has long disappeared and been replaced by a Commonwealth of equal partners.

C A *Punch* cartoon shows Benjamin Disraeli, the British Prime Minister, holding an important key

"NIXON'S NAVIGATION"
SMOKELESS STEAM COAL

Proprietors—
NIXON'S NAVIGATION CO., LTD.,
Registered Office : BUTE DOCKS, CARDIFF.
London Office : 5, FENCHURCH STREET, E.C.

Shippers of the well-known
"NIXON'S NAVIGATION"
SMOKELESS STEAM COAL

which has been used for the TRIALS OF SPEED of HIS MAJESTY'S WAR VESSELS, and on board the ROYAL YACHTS, for many years.

It is also extensively used by FOREIGN GOVERNMENTS, and the principal BRITISH & FOREIGN STEAMSHIP AND RAILWAY COMPANIES, also by Steam Launches, Motors, Electrical Works, and for Bunker purposes.

"NIXON'S NAVIGATION"
Large & Small Washed Steam Nuts
are also highly appreciated by users
- - - of Steam Power. - - -

The Coals can be shipped at the principal Ports
in the Bristol Channel.

xxxvi
INSOLES LIMITED

Proprietors of
Cymmer Merthyr
Smokeless Steam Coal

SUPPLIED TO THE PRINCIPAL STEAMSHIP LINES AND TO THE PRINCIPAL COALING DEPOTS IN THE MEDI-TERRANEAN, EAST, SOUTH AMERICA, BRAZILS, ETC.

On the ADMIRALTY LIST for
Use in the BRITISH NAVY.

Insoles No. 2 Rhondda Coal
Particularly Recommended for Bunkers.

Sole Shipping Agents :
Geo. Insole and Son,
Bute Docks, CARDIFF.

Telegraphic Address—INSOLES, CARDIFF.

... the British Empire is ... the greatest instrument for good the world has ever seen.

D A statement made by Lord Curzon, Under Secretary for India, in 1894

E *(left)* Advertisements by Welsh coal exporters boast of their connection with shipping lines and the Royal Navy

---

1 Look at the map of the British Empire (source A).
   (a) Can you see any patterns?
   (b) Can you suggest reasons why these types of places may have become part of the British Empire rather than other places?

2 What do the battle and campaign names on source B tell us about where Welsh soldiers served during this period?

3 Using information in this and other chapters, say why you think so many Welsh people went to various parts of the Empire?

4 Can you imagine any ways in which improvements in technology changed the Empire and the ideas people had about it?

5 'Lord Curzon cannot be serious in source D. There is no way that anyone can sensibly praise what the British did.'
   (a) Do you agree with this statement?
   (b) Why might people at the time have taken Lord Curzon seriously?

6 Why would it not be so easy for any country to build up an empire today?

23 *I*reland – 'The Great Hunger'

No man can stop the disease nor can any man be certain that a single potato will remain in the island at the end of a few months. Two thirds of the peasants have nothing, absolutely nothing ... they must die by the million.

A James Burns's letter of 1845, to the Duke of Wellington in London

... of a population of 240, I found thirteen already dead from want. The survivors were like walking skeletons ... the children crying with pain, the women too weak to stand.

B A report by the politician W E Forster, after a visit to the village of Bundorragha in County Mayo

C Ragged Irishmen watch a funeral at Skibbereen during the famine

Like the Welsh, the Irish are a Celtic people. Their language and many of their customs are similar. For centuries, Ireland was under English rule. During the seventeenth century, many English and Scottish families were encouraged to settle in Ireland. They made their homes in the north east of the country, in an area called Ulster. The majority of the Irish people were Roman Catholics but the newcomers were Protestants, most being members of the Church of England. At the start of the nineteenth century, the whole of Ireland was a part of Great Britain and was governed from London.

The ordinary Irish people were small farmers or crofters. They were poor and because of their poverty they depended on potatoes for their food. The Protestants enjoyed better standards of living and were in control. The Irish longed for the day when their country would be free from foreign rule. In Parliament, it was difficult for them to make their views known because a law prevented Roman Catholics from being MPs. Thanks to Daniel O'Connell, this law was changed in 1829.

'The Great Famine'

It was said that the average Irishman ate over four kilos of potatoes daily. It was a reasonable if monotonous diet. In 1844, the Irish potato crop was attacked by a **blight**. The blight returned the following year and, as food became scarce, so families began to starve.

Without potatoes and with no money to buy other food, the people became desperate. As the workhouses filled, mobs attacked places where food was known to be stored. Some even attempted to eat grass and the bark from trees.

Sums of money were raised in England to send help, and food centres were set up, but the problem was so serious it could not be solved by charity. The answer was to send cheap wheat and other grain to Ireland to make bread, but this could not be done. Corn Laws had been passed which stopped grain coming into the country from abroad until the price rose above a certain level. Robert Peel, the Prime Minister, wanted to change the law but the Tory landowners refused. They feared that cheap grain would flood into the country from abroad and cut their profits. The danger of millions starving meant that Peel could wait no longer. He went against the wishes of his own party and set aside the law. Sadly, the ending of the Corn Laws came too late to do much good. The potato crop failed again the following year and once more in 1848.

After the Great Famine

It is reckoned that 1 million Irish people died of disease and starvation. Many emigrated, some coming to England and Wales, and another 1 million crossed the Atlantic Ocean to America. They took with them bitter memories and a hatred of the English who had allowed them to starve. Cottages were left and whole villages became deserted as starvation and emigration reduced the population of Ireland from 8 million to 6 million.

The suffering of Ireland did not end there. When many Catholic crofters could not pay their rents to their English landlords they were turned out of their homes. Afterwards, their cottages were burned down to prevent them returning as squatters.

Captain Boycott, a land agent, was ignored, treated with contempt and had to leave Ireland. **Boycotting** became a very powerful weapon. In America, Irish immigrants formed the Fenian Brotherhood. The aim of the society was to drive the English from Ireland. They were prepared to use violence to bring it about. The real troubles were about to begin.

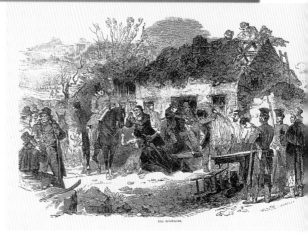

E   An artist's impression of the eviction of a family from their home in 1848

You must shun him on the roadside … on the street … in the shop … in the market place, and even in the place of worship; by leaving him alone, as if he were a leper of old, you must show him your detestation of the crime he has committed.

F   The Irish leader, Charles Stewart Parnell, told his people how to treat the landlords and their agents

I … swear allegiance to the Irish Republic … and will do my very utmost, at every risk, while life lasts, to defend its independence … so help me God.

D   The deserted village of Moveen in 1849

G   Part of the oath taken by Fenians

---

1   Look at sources A and B. If the British Government had been genuinely concerned about the problem, why was very little done to help the Irish people?

2   Look at sources C, D and E. What impressions are the artists trying to give in each of these sources?

3   If you had been an Irish peasant farmer, what decisions might you have taken during this period?

4   Do you think the advice given to the Irish people in source F is likely to have been successful? Give reasons for your answer.

5   Does the information provided in this chapter help to explain why there have been problems in Ireland in recent times? Can you find any links between these events in the nineteenth century and the ideas, beliefs and events of the last few years?

'United we stand'

... all contracts between any workmen for obtaining an advance of wages ... or lessening their usual hours of time working ... shall be declared void.

A An Act of 1800

My lord, if we have violated any law, it was not done intentionally, we have injured no man's reputation; we were uniting to protect our wives and our children from starvation. We challenge any man ... to prove that we have acted different ...

B A part of George Loveless's statement

C (below) A cartoon of the time makes fun of people who joined unions

The idea of workers joining together in order to be better placed in getting a fair deal from their masters, was not new. At the end of the eighteenth century, men who tried to 'combine' were seen as a threat and treated as trouble makers. The government passed laws, the Combination Acts, which made trade unions illegal.

In 1825, the Combination Acts were removed and immediately trade unions sprang up all over the country. Robert Owen thought it best to have workers brought together in one large union. He named his union, the Grand National Consolidated Trades Union. Being a bit of a mouthful, it was called the Grand National or GNCTU for short. Owen's plan was ambitious. Employers became scared as membership rose to over half a million. Factory owners threatened to sack men who joined the union. In 1834, came the case of the six farm labourers from Tolpuddle.

The Tolpuddle Martyrs

Tolpuddle is a small village in Dorset. In 1834, six local farm workers decided to join a union. They were the brothers George and James Loveless, their brother-in-law and his son, Thomas and John Stanfield, John Brine (who was courting their sister) and an outsider, James Hammett. Although trade unions were allowed by law, they were arrested. Membership of the union required taking part in a ceremony which included repeating an **oath**. Their employer took advantage of an old law which said that taking oaths was illegal. They were not charged with being members of a union but with being involved in taking illegal oaths. The men were not

Yes Gentlemen, these is my principles,—no K—g,—no L—ds,—no Parsons,—no Police,—no Taxes.

allowed to give evidence but a statement written by George Loveless was read out in court. At the end of their trial in Dorchester, they were all found guilty and sentenced to be transported to Tasmania for seven years. Immediately there was uproar. A fund was opened to support their wives and children and a campaign started to get them set free. Those who led the fight were Robert Owen, William Cobbett and Daniel O'Connell.

After four years, the men were allowed to return home. Five of the six chose to emigrate to Canada and only one, James Hammett, decided to live in Tolpuddle. He died in the Dorchester workhouse in 1891 at the age of 90. The punishment of the six farm workers cooled enthusiasm for trade unions. Men would hesitate to join unions if they risked transportation. Robert Owen's GNCTU came to an end.

New types of trade unions

The experience of the GNCTU led men to be more cautious. New, smaller unions appeared, each for a different type of skilled worker. These were better organised with paid officials and were now known as new model unions. The following years were quiet until, during the 1880s, more defiant unions appeared again.

God is our guide! No swords we draw,
We kindle not war's battle fires;
By reason, union, justice, law,
We claim the birthright of our sires;
We raise the watchword, liberty,
We will, we will, we will be free.

D George Loveless, who was a part-time Methodist preacher, wrote this poem

E *(below) The Returned 'Convicts',* featured in *Cleave's Penny Gazette of Variety* (1838)

THE RETURNED ' CONVICTS '

James Brine
Aged 25

Thomas Stanfield
Aged 51

John Stanfield
Aged 25

George Loveless
Aged 41

James Loveless
Aged 29

1 Look at sources A and C.
   (a) Why should the government want to pass an Act like the one referred to in source A?
   (b) What evidence is there that the artist in source C did not approve of people joining unions?

2 (a) What do you think the Government wanted to achieve by pursuing the case of the Tolpuddle Martyrs?
   (b) Did they achieve their aims?

3 Look at sources B and D. Can you see any differences in the points George Loveless is trying to make in the two sources?

As Far Off as Ever.

A A cartoon in the *Western Mail* (1898) shows the different views of mine owners and their workmen on the issue of pay

B Bryant and May's match girls on strike in 1888

Further disputes

The pay of Welsh miners – a sliding scale

During the 1870s, less coal was required and as its price fell, so pit owners cut the pay of miners. There were several strikes but, in the end, the miners had to give in and accept lower wages. The miners' leader was William Abraham. He was generally known by his bardic name, 'Mabon'. A big man, he was a great speaker and had a fine tenor voice. He was fond of singing Welsh hymns and was proud of the Welsh language. In 1885, he was elected Liberal MP for the Rhondda and dared to speak Welsh in the House of Commons. When some found it funny and laughed, Abraham informed them that he had been reciting the Lord's Prayer. Mabon tried to bring peace to the coalfield and it was due to his efforts that miners agreed to have their wages paid according to a **sliding scale**. The scale depended on the price of coal and the profit made.

Match girls and the London dockers

Then came two strikes which attracted the attention of the nation. In 1888, lowly paid girls who worked at the factory of the London match-makers, Bryant and May, walked out. Their work involved dipping matchsticks in phosphorus. To speed their work up, they held the matchsticks between their lips. If their mouths came in contact with the phosphorus, it caused an unsightly condition known as 'phossy-jaw'. The girls had a lot of public support and won their case for better working conditions. The following year, London dockers demanded an increase in pay which would give them 2p an hour. In the currency of that time, this was sixpence (nicknamed 'a **tanner**'). Again there was great public support for the dockers. A strike fund was set up and money poured in, some of it from as far away as Australia. In the end, the employers gave in and paid up.

Trouble on the Taff Vale Railway

The Taff Vale Railway Company got on well with its workers. It was one of the first companies to pay pensions to them when they retired. In spite of this, like all other railway companies, it was against its employees joining the railwaymen's union, the Amalgamated Society of Railway Servants. In 1900, there was a railway strike which lasted for ten days. During that time, the railway owners brought in workers from outside, **blackleg** labour. When the strike was over, the company took the union to court and claimed back all the money lost because of the strike. The court found in favour of the Taff Vale Railway and the union had to pay the company £23,000. This meant that from now on, any union calling a strike could end up in court and be forced to pay a heavy fine which might make it bankrupt.

Afterwards, relations between workers and their employers got even worse and there were a great many strikes. At the same time, a new political party appeared to challenge the Conservatives and Liberals and look after the interest of working-class people.

STRIKE !
ON THE
Taff Vale Railway.

Men's Headquarters,
Cobourn Street.
Cathays.

There has been a strike on the Taff Vale Railway since Monday last. The Management are using every means to decoy men here who they employ for the purpose of black-legging the men on strike.

Drivers, Firemen, Guards, Brakesmen, and
SIGNALMEN, are all out.

Are you willing to be known as a

Blackleg ?

If you accept employment on the Taff Vale, that is what you will be known by. On arriving at Cardiff, call at the above address, where you can get information and assistance.

RICHARD BELL,
General Secretary.

C A poster used in 1900 at the time of the Taff Vale Railway strike

If any row threatened, Mabon never tried to restore order in any usual way. He promptly struck up a Welsh hymn or *Land of my Fathers*. Hardly had he reached the second line when, with uplifted arms, he had the vast crowd accompanying him like a trained choir. The storm had passed.

D A Scottish miners' leader explains Mabon's secret. From *South Wales Miners*, by R Page Arnot (1967)

The dockers were brilliantly led. Each day, with bands and banners, they marched through London … As well as banners, on one occasion the marchers carried stinking onions, old fish heads and rotten pieces of meat stuck on spikes, to show the more wealthy people of London what the dockers lived on.

E A description of the docker's struggle in *The Labour Party*, by Edward Wilmot

Sing a song of sixpence,
Dockers on the strike,
Guinea pigs as hungry,
As the greedy pike.
Till the docks are opened,
Burns for you will speak,
Courage lads, and you'll win,
Well within a week.

F The striking dockers' song which they sang on their marches

1 Look at sources A, C and D.
  (a) What point is the artist trying to make in source A?
  (b) How reliable do you think source D is? Give reasons for your answer.
  (c) Does source D tell us anything about attitudes at this time?
  (d) Whose side does the poster in source C seem to be supporting?

2 Which developments in this chapter seem:
  (a) The most helpful in improving the power of the trade unions?
  (b) The least helpful in improving the power of the trade unions?

𝓛iberals and the rise of Labour

A verse from Gilbert and Sullivan's *Iolanthe* ran:

> *Every boy and every gal*
> *That's born into this world alive,*
> *Is either a little Liberal*
> *Or else a little Conservative.*

This would certainly not have been true when the opera was written in 1882. Though some changes had taken place, few working people in the industrial towns had the right to vote.

An act of Parliament passed in 1867 doubled the number of men who could vote. After 1872, voting at election time was to be by secret ballot. In 1884, the vote was given to men over the age of 21. This meant that every miner, steel worker and farm hand could vote. The question was who would they vote for?

Great days for the Liberals

As there was no party which served the interests of working people alone, most of the new voters supported the Liberals. Already, the people of Merthyr Tydfil and the Rhondda had sent Henry Richard and William Abraham to Parliament. In the elections of 1885, the Liberals won 30 out of the 34 Welsh seats. Even Sir Watkin Wynn, whose family had sent a Member to Parliament for 182 years, was defeated! Five years later, the people of Caernarvon boroughs elected a local solicitor as their MP, his name was David Lloyd George. In time, he was to become the first Welshman to hold the

---

Few save the poor feel for the poor, the rich know not how hard it is to be needful of food. I ask you therefore to return to parliament a man of yourselves who, being poor, can feel for the poor …

 A Keir Hardie's words when he first stood for Parliament in 1888

He drove up to the House … in a stained working suit with a cloth cap on his head and accompanied by a noisy brass band followed by a noisy crowd from the dockland slums which included many undesirable elements … and revolutionaries who should be driven from our shores before they infect our good and sensible working people.

B A newspaper describes Keir Hardie's arrival at the House of Commons. Quoted in *The Hungry Heart - James Keir Hardie*, by John Cockburn (1956)

C *(right)* An election poster of 1892 supporting Keir Hardie

VOTE FOR

Home Rule.

Democratic Government.

Justice to Labour

No Monopoly.

No Landlordism

Temperance Reform.

Healthy Homes.

Fair Rents.

Eight-Hour Day.

Work for the Unemployed.

KEIR HARDIE.

office of Prime Minister. Many of the Welsh Liberal MPs were Nonconformists. They wanted to remove the influence of the Anglican church and protect the culture and language of Wales.

Keir Hardie

Born near Glasgow in 1856, Keir Hardie was one of nine children. His family were very poor and, from the age of twelve, he worked in a Scottish pit. He taught himself to read and write and became active in trade union affairs. As a champion of working people and the poor, he did not want to depend on the Liberals. In 1893, he formed the Independent Labour Party. The people of Lanark did not elect him when he first stood, but four years later the voters of East Ham in London did.

Some newspapers sneered at Hardie and called him 'the Member for the Unemployed'. He was proud of the nickname. In 1893, he showed his annoyance when the papers paid more attention to a royal birth than it did to another event which happened on the same day - a mining disaster which claimed the lives of 290 at Cilfynydd in Wales. His attitude upset many and he lost his seat at East Ham. In 1900, he made a come back when he was returned to the House of Commons as the Member for Merthyr Tydfil.

In the election of 1906, 29 Labour MPs were returned to Parliament, a mere handful compared with the 377 Liberals and 157 Conservatives. In Wales, not a single Conservative was returned, but it was to be a further 20 years before 'Wales belonged to the Labour Party'.

E A cartoon entitled 'The Member for the Unemployed'

I take it that this House is the mouthpiece of the nation as a whole ... for the unemployed equally as for the well-to-do classes. But this House will not be speaking in the name of the nation ... if something is not done for those people whose sufferings are so great and for whom I plead.

D Hardie's maiden (first) speech in the House of Commons

Given a strong lead, the Welsh people will place themselves at the head of the Socialist movement. Kindly by nature, genial one to another, loving justice, and hating oppression, they can easily be roused to battle for the right.

F An article by Hardie in the *Labour Leader* (1898)

1 Look at sources A, C, D and F.
  (a) How did Keir Hardie try to gain the support of the people?
  (b) What kinds of people would you expect to be opposed to his views?

2 Look at sources B and E.
  (a) What evidence is there that the newspaper disapproves of Hardie and what he stands for?
  (b) Is source E for or against Hardie? Give reasons for your answer.

3 What reasons can you suggest as to why the Welsh people gave little support to the Conservative Party after 1867?

26 Fighting disease and pain

The man who is on the operating table in one of our hospitals is in far greater danger of dying than was a soldier on the battlefield at Waterloo.

A James Simpson, speaking about operations of the time

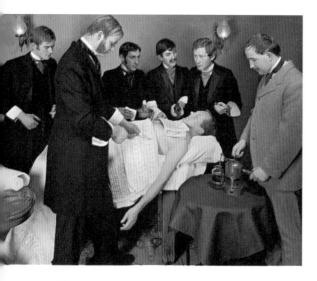

B An operation as it would have taken place in Lister's day. Note the dress of the doctors and the use of both anaesthetics and antiseptics

C (*right*) A contemporary cartoon makes fun of Jenner's idea of vaccination

Although they were on the way out, the old quacksalvers ('quacks') and barber-surgeons (with red and white poles outside their shops) could still be found. They used simple, sometimes useless and often painful remedies to treat the sick. Hot irons to clean wounds and blood letting (opening of veins or using **leeches**) were two ways of treating illness. Operations were a gruesome business. Limbs were amputated without pain-killing **anaesthetics** or any regard for the needs of hygiene. The chances were that even if the poor victim survived the agony of surgery, he would die from infection afterwards. Fortunately, there were also good doctors and some highly regarded surgeons and **physicians**.

The cries of agony associated with surgery were **horrendous** to hear. Sir Humphry Davy, the man who invented the miners' safety lamp, also discovered that nitrous oxide could be used to numb the senses and make people unconscious. The fact that it made people giggle earned it the nickname 'laughing-gas'. Far better was chloroform. First discovered by James Simpson, it was both safe and easy to use. One clergyman spoke out against the use of anaesthetics and called them the work of the devil since they were designed to, 'rob God of the deep, earnest cries in times of troubles for help'!

It was Joseph Lister who first used **antiseptics** to make surgery safer. During operations, he allowed a weak solution of carbolic acid to be sprayed into the area around the operating table. He also insisted that his instruments were placed in boiling water. Although some found his insistence on cleanliness amusing, his methods were soon used in all hospitals.

Smallpox was a very contagious disease. People who survived it were left with their faces dreadfully scarred or pock-marked. Edward Jenner heard of an old wives' tale which said that dairymaids seldom caught smallpox. He investigated and discovered that they caught cowpox instead. He came to the

conclusion that harmless cowpox gave them immunity from harmful smallpox. Afterwards, Jenner injected people with a substance taken from infected calves to protect them from smallpox. At first, few were convinced of the safety of his methods and he faced a lot of opposition and even ridicule. Later, he was handsomely rewarded for his work by the government.

After further work by the French scientist, Louis Pasteur, other vaccines were developed which gave protection against diseases such as cholera, typhoid and diptheria, which killed many children. He had, in fact, discovered the principle of vaccination (*vaccus* is Latin for a cow). People given mild doses of a disease would become immune to a more serious attack of that same disease.

War often brings about advances in medical science. The Crimean War (1851-56) saw the start of the first well organised nursing service. This was the work of one of the most famous women in British history, Florence Nightingale.

'The Lady with the Lamp'

Florence Nightingale was no ordinary woman. At a time when nursing was considered an unsuitable occupation for young ladies, she went against the wishes of her family and those in authority, assembled a team of nurses and sailed for the Crimea. There, she found conditions quite appalling (see source D).

Nightingale completely changed the conditions. Her nightly check of the wards led grateful soldiers to call her 'The Lady with the Lamp'. On her return to Britain, she became the authority on the management of hospitals and the training of nurses. The nursing service of today remains largely based on the guidelines she laid down.

> *The filth was indescribable. The men in the corridors lay on unwashed floors crawling with vermin. There were no pillows ... men lay with their heads on their boots wrapped in blankets stiff with blood and filth ... Amputations were carried out in the full sight of patients.*

 D Florence Nightingale, writing of conditions on her arrival in the Crimea

F. N.

BORN 12 MAY 1820.

DIED 13 AUGUST 1910.

 E *(right)* The grave of Florence Nightingale at East Willow in Hampshire. It was her wish that her headstone should bear only her initials

---

1 What information is given in this chapter to support the opinion of Simpson in source A?

2 Look at sources C and D.
   (a) From what evidence might the cartoonist in source C have obtained their information?
   (b) What is wrong with the conditions described in source D?

3 'Those responsible for advances in medicine did not always have an easy time convincing others.' How much evidence can you find in this chapter to support this statement?

4 Of the medical improvements referred to in this chapter, which do you feel was most useful in the long term? Give reasons for your answer.

5 Using the information in this chapter, why would a patient be more likely to survive at the end of this period (1914) than at the beginning (1760)?

27 *W*riters, musicians and poets

The Victorian age produced many famous writers - Robert Louis Stevenson who wrote *Treasure Island*, Thomas Hardy, famous for *Far From the Madding Crowd* and *Tess of the D'Urbervilles*, and the author of the Sherlock Holmes stories, Sir Arthur Conan Doyle. Some wrote about the everyday lives of ordinary people and much of what we know about life at that time comes from their stories. The most famous of these was Charles Dickens.

Dickens was born in Portsmouth where his father worked as a clerk in the Naval Pay Office. When the family moved to Kent, his father ran into debt and ended up in a debtors' prison. With all the family's possessions pawned, the young Charles had to leave school. He found a job in a blacking factory where he worked twelve hours a day for 30p a week. Lonely, hungry and ashamed, he became determined to succeed. For a while he worked as a reporter and wrote articles under his brother's nickname, Boz. His first book was *Pickwick Papers* and afterwards his novels came thick and fast. In his books, he exposed the evils of the time and described the harshness and cruelty of the lives of the poor. As his reputation grew, Charles Dickens became a rich and much travelled man. Another novelist who knew poverty at first hand was the Welshman, Daniel Owen.

Owen came from Mold in Clwyd. He was only a few months old when his father and two brothers were drowned in a mining accident. Afterwards he lived in poverty, had little schooling and was finally apprenticed to a tailor. Owen then decided to prepare himself for the ministry and went to college at Bala. He gave it up and returned to tailoring, starting his own draper's business, but this came to an end when his health broke down. Owen's novels were about Welsh life and the chapel. One, *Rhys Lewis*, is largely based on his life. Even though Welsh people were more inclined to read

Pawnshops, Sketches by Boz

Debtors' prisons, Pickwick Papers

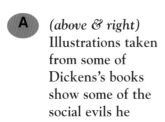

A *(above & right)* Illustrations taken from some of Dickens's books show some of the social evils he wrote about

Workhouse children, Oliver Twist

Private schools, Nicholas Nickleby

the Bible than novels, his books became popular. He has been called 'the greatest Welsh novelist'.

One Welshman who did achieve worldwide fame was the musician and composer, Joseph Parry. Born in Merthyr Tydfil in 1841, Parry's home was a two-up, two-down workman's cottage. As a boy, he worked down the pit before joining his father at the Cyfarthfa Ironworks. In the 1850s, the Parry family emigrated to the United States. For the next twelve years, Joseph Parry worked in the ironworks at Danville, Pennyslvania and took music lessons in his spare time. Backed by money from well-wishers, he returned home to study at the Royal College of Music in London. He was thirty-one when he was appointed Professor of Music at Aberystwyth. Although he wrote many choruses and hymns, he is best remembered for the hymn tune Aberystwyth (still a firm favourite in chapels) and the much loved tune Myfanwy.

The *eisteddfod*

The word eisteddfod means a meeting of poets. The tradition of the eisteddfod goes back over centuries and has come to mean a festival with all types of literary and musical activities and competitions. For a time, eisteddfodau ceased but, in the 1820s, they were revived and became very popular. Schools and chapels held local eisteddfodau which included competitions for singing, poetry and recitation. The standards were not always high but eisteddfodau allowed ordinary people to enjoy themselves.

In 1858, the National Eisteddfod was revived when it was held at Llangollen. With Bards of the Gorsedd dressed in fine robes and presided over by the Archdruid, it was to become the main festival of its kind. The winning of the bardic chair was a much prized honour.

C   A photograph of Daniel Owen

Although he habitually spoke English in Welsh company because he thought it grand to do so, Joseph Parry never escaped his roots ... he was without doubt the most well known Welshman in the world at the beginning of the twentieth century.

D   A contemporary view of Joseph Parry

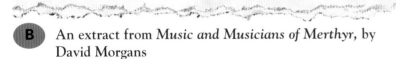

Dr Parry was without doubt the greatest musical genius that Wales has ever produced ...

B   An extract from *Music and Musicians of Merthyr,* by David Morgans

---

1 'Because they wrote fiction, authors such as Stevenson, Conan Doyle and Dickens are of no use to the historian.' Do you agree with this statement?

2 Look at source A.
 (a) What messages do these pictures appear to give?
 (b) Do these messages agree with or disagree with any of the information given elsewhere in this book?

3 (a) 'Some of the best writers and musicians faced difficult lives themselves and used their difficulties in their work.' Is there anything to support this view in this chapter?
 (b) What helps to make a writer, artist or musician become well known? This may not be as simple to answer as it seems.

4 What factors led to the revival of the *eisteddfod* at this particular time?

28

Entertainment and sport

> We bowled iron hoops on the pavement, spun tops, blew soap bubbles ... played marbles, leap frog, I spy. At school, we played rounders ... and 'bat and catty' ... girls skipped and hopped on the pavement and played duckstones.

A From *Rhymney Memories* by T Jones (1938)

B The programme at The Empire, Tonypandy (1909) and a poster listing the acts at The Palace, Cardiff (1911)

Most people, even the less well off, found time to enjoy some social life. Working men had **allotments** and enjoyed keeping pigeons, ferrets and whippets. They also joined male voice choirs, glee clubs and brass bands. For children, there were lots of play activities. (See source A).

The music halls

Every town of any size had a music hall. The cheapest seats were in the balcony, 'the gods' as they were called. For as little as 1p you could get a good evening's entertainment.

Picture palaces and silent films

At the beginning of the twentieth century the first cinemas showed silent films with music provided by a pianist who sat at the front. Ten or more short films could be seen for 1p (it cost 2p if you wanted to sit in the best seats, the grand circle).

The Bracchis

During the 1880's, several Italian families set up businesses in South Wales. They made and sold ice-cream and opened cafes. Names such as **Bracchi**, Berni, Conti, Carpanini, Fulgoni and Rossi appeared above cafes in the high streets of most Valley towns. They were very popular meeting places.

Newspapers, magazines and comics

With more people able to read, more newspapers and magazines were sold. The *Western Mail* appeared in 1869. In 1896, George Harmsworth started the first truly popular national daily paper, the *Daily Mail*, and a magazine for children appeared in 1890, it was called *Comic Cuts*. Afterwards, all children's magazines were called comics.

Sport

James Alfred Bevan may not be a rugby legend like Gareth Edwards and Ieuan Evans, yet, on 19 February 1881, he led the very first Welsh international rugby team. The match was played against England at Blackheath in London but sadly England won! One of the oldest rugby clubs in Wales is Mountain Ash. There is a story that the club's nickname, the 'Old Firm', came from the cry of a hawker who sold fruit outside the ground - 'Come and buy from the old firm.'

In those days, football was more popular than rugby in Wales and football matches drew even larger crowds than today. One of Wales's great footballers was Chirk-born Billy Meredith. From the age of twelve he worked in a local pit and continued to work there even after he had signed for Manchester City! He played until he was fifty years old and won 48 Welsh caps. It is said that he always played with a tooth-pick in his mouth.

... in my home town we congregated ... to listen to our friends who had just started work in the colliery. The amount of money spent by these young stags was really very small, things being so cheap ... a packet of cigarettes could be bought for a penny. Our Italian only tolerated us if things were going well ... if anything upset him ... he would bawl from across the counter ... and we had to clear out.

C Walter Davies recalled his visits to a Bracchi in Bedlinog. Quoted in *Ups and Downs*, by Walter Davies (1975)

☆ THE IMPERIAL 占
Picture Palace
Proprietors : THE CARDIFF & DISTRICT ELECTRIC THEATRES, Ltd.
Head Offices: Charing Cross House, 29a Charing Cross Road, W.C.

53 & 55 QUEEN STREET, CARDIFF.
General Manager   W. REYNOLDS-BENJAMIN

Telephone, 2578 Cardiff.

This Handsome

PICTURE HOUSE
Open Daily,
from 2 until 11 p.m.

The Imperial ORCHESTRA
OF SPECIALLY SELECTED

BRITISH MUSICIANS
PERFORM DAILY.

AFTERNOON TEAS from
3.30 to 5.30, FREE.

The most Up-to-Date Theatre, with its Beautifully Furnished Lounge. 4,000 Cubic feet space.
THE COOLEST THEATRE IN SUMMER.
THE COSIEST IN WINTER.

Prices: 3d., 6d. & 1/-.   ENTIRE CHANGE OF PROGRAMME ON MONDAYS AND THEURSDAYS.

featured orchestras. The Imperial Picture Palace closed down as the New Imperial Cinema on 25 April 1936 and reopened after reconstruction on 14 September 1936 as the Odeon with a striking green facade. The opening film was Charlie Chaplin in 'Modern Times'

D An advertisement for The Imperial Picture Palace in Cardiff

E Part of the front page of an early edition of the *Western Mail*

F The very first Welsh international rugby team in 1881

---

1 **In what ways did the leisure of working people differ at this time from that of today?**

2 **Do the sources and other information provided here tell us anything about leisure activities for women?**

3 (a) **Can you think of any types of leisure and entertainment which have not been covered in this chapter?**

   (b) **Why do you think they may not have been included? There could be several reasons you might refer to.**

29

Change and continuity

A   A view of Pontypridd in 1865

The Welsh language is the curse of Wales. Their old language shrouds them in darkness. For all purposes, Welsh is a dead language.

B   By 1866, this article had appeared in *The Times*

Welsh nationality has survived two thousand years in spite of every effort to crush out its vitality. Still, after all, we are still here.

C   An extract from a speech by David Lloyd George, the young Welsh-speaking MP for Caernarfon

This book has described many of the changes which occurred between 1760 and 1914. These changes took place so slowly that people were not aware of them at the time. Towards the end of their lives, men and women may have looked back and remembered things as they had been in their childhood. A few very old people might have even spoken of 'the good old days'- a time before the pits, tips and rows of terraced houses, when the valleys were green and wooded.

Looking at old pictures is a good way of studying the past. In the picture of Pontypridd (source A) you can see many of the changes which had turned a small village into a busy town. Situated at the point where the Rivers Taff and Rhondda met, and midway between Merthyr Tydfil and Cardiff, by 1865 Pontypridd was an important industrial centre. It was served by both the Glamorgan Canal and the Taff Vale Railway.

Welsh language and culture

Long ago, in the twelfth century, the Bishop of St David's sent a letter to the Pope. In it he said, 'The Welsh are entirely different in nation, laws and habits, judgements and customs.' But by 1900, the proportion of Welsh-speaking people in Wales was less than 50 per cent and it was to fall even lower. English laws had long applied to Wales but now as people moved to Wales to find work in the industrial areas, so English became the language more commonly used. It was really a marvel that the language and culture of Wales had managed to survive at all.

A new national awareness

Some had never given up the struggle to maintain the national identity of Wales and remind the Welsh people that they were a separate race with a culture and history of their own. In 1856, father and son, Evan and James James, composed *Hen Wlad fy Nhadau* (Land of my Fathers). The song expressed the feelings of the Welsh people about their homeland. It was very popular and became the Welsh national anthem. In 1886, a movement called *Cymru Fydd* (Young Wales) was formed to fight for self-government. For a number of years the movement was strong but there were disagreements and the movement collapsed.

The challenge was next taken up by Welsh Members of Parliament. In 1900 and again in 1906, the Liberals won all the seats in Wales, except at Merthyr Tydfil where the popular socialist Keir Hardie remained the MP. People like Tom Ellis made sure that Welsh issues such as questions of land ownership, were raised in Parliament.

David Lloyd George first made his name as a defender of the rights of Welsh Nonconformists. Later, he became a figure of national importance. As Chancellor of the Exchequer, he was largely responsible for providing pensions for the old and benefits for those who were sick or unemployed. In 1916, he became Prime Minister - the first Welshman to hold this office.

The new feeling of national pride led to the setting up of a number of important Welsh institutions. In 1893, the university colleges at Aberystwyth, Bangor and Cardiff were brought together to form the University of Wales. Then, in 1907, royal charters were granted for the founding of a National Library and a National Museum. The decision to hold a National Eisteddfod every year helped to promote the Welsh language further and more Welsh books, plays and poems appeared.

Reflecting on their lives
And what did those people who looked back over their lives really feel? As shown below, they had different memories.

E A *Punch* cartoon of 1910 shows that Lloyd George, in spite of his fame, has not forgotten his Welsh background

All our social life was all with the chapel. Because there was something every night of the week for us ... in our chapel. Everyone went to chapel then. That was our way of life. And it wasn't dull, mind ... As far as I'm concerned every colliery can close ... they hold very bad memories ... but those were the very times when people clung. Clung to each other.

Good old days they were. Happy days.

D The recollections of a Llwynypia woman

F A Penygraig miner saw things quite differently

1 **Looking back over this book:**
(a) **What do you think is the change which may have had the greatest effect on:**
   i) **working men;**
   ii) **women;**
   iii) **children;**
   iv) **wealthy people?**
(b) **Which event do you think people at the time would have most:**
   (i) **approved of;**
   (ii) **disapproved of?**
(c) **What do you think might have been the greatest change that working people may have noticed in their living conditions?**
(d) **Can you think of any aspects of life which hardly changed at all during this period?**
(e) **Are there some changes you think happened by accident or chance?**
   If so, which?
(f) **Are there any major changes which you think happened almost completely because of the work of one person? If so, which?**

2 **If you were allowed just 100 words to describe the main changes which happened during this period, what would you write?**

3 **In most periods there are winners and losers. Who do you think were the main winners and losers in this book? Explain the reasons for your choices.**

4 (a) **Was Wales a better place in 1914 than in 1760?**
   (b) **Was the Welsh identity stronger in 1914 than it had been during the previous century? Give reasons for your answers.**

Glossary

abolished brought to an end
allotments pieces of land cultivated by people in their spare time
anaesthetic a substance which causes loss of feeling
Anglican member of the Church of England
antiseptic substance which kills germs
apprentice a person learning a trade
aqueduct a bridge which carries water

Bastille fortress in Paris used as a prison
black-leg person who continues to work when others are on strike
blight disease which attacks and destroys plants
boffin slang for a brainy scientist
boycotting refusing to have anything to do with
Bracchis Italian-owned cafés
butty slang for a friend (similar to American 'buddy')

choke-damp suffocating gas found in mines (carbon-monoxide)
cholera infectious disease, caught by drinking polluted water
clipper fast sailing ship
colony country ruled by another country
Combination Acts laws which banned trade unions
commissioner official appointed to do a particular job
common land land freely used by common people
commune a group of people, not of one family, sharing accommodation and goods
corrupt dishonest, willing to take a bribe
Court of Requests court before which debtors were brought

dysentery disease similar to severe diarrhoea

endowed supported by a gift of money
epidemic outbreak of a disease which attacks many people at the same time

fallow land being rested after growing crops
fire-damp explosive gas found in mines (methane)
folklore old stories and beliefs which have been passed down

gallows wooden frame for hanging criminals
guillotine machine used to execute people by cutting off their heads

horrendous dreadful or horrible

leeches blood sucking slug-like creatures
lime kiln furnace used to make lime
loom machine for weaving cloth
Luddites weavers who broke machines

militant inclined to take violent action
mill textile factory
mutilation badly injured by having limbs cut off

navvies shortened form of Navigators; men who dug canals and later built the railways

oath promise one swears to keep
overseer a person who oversees others

parasites insects such as fleas and lice
parish district with its own church
pauper very poor person
pawn shop shop that lends money against items left with the owner (pawn broker)
pneumoconiosis disease caught by inhaling dust
physician doctor who uses medicines
piece-rate payment according to how much has been made
privies lavatories

radical person who believes in solving problems by getting to the real, or root, cause
raw materials natural materials which are used to make other things

Riot Act statement read as a warning to rioters
rotary engine engine that can turn a wheel
Royal Commission body of people set up to look into a matter
satanic evil and unpleasant
scolding telling off
scurvy disease caused by lack of fresh vegetables (Vitamin C)
silicosis disease caught by inhaling dust
sliding scale level of pay which moves up and down (according to the price of coal)
sludge slimy mud
slump time when business is bad
smelting heating iron ore to get the metal from it
snuff powdered tobacco
suffrage the vote or the right to vote

tanner slang name for a sixpenny coin
tenant farmer farmer who rents his land
tommy shops name given to shops owned by factory owners
transported (as a punishment) being sent to a convict settlement abroad
truck system paying men part of their wages in tokens instead of money

void useless or invalid

whitewashed painted with a mixture of lime and water
willow-patterned a blue design with Chinese figures